DISARM DAILY CONFLICT

Your Life Depends On It

CHRIS ROBERTS

Cover design by 100Covers.com
Formatted by FormattedBooks.com

FREE SAFE RESOURCES

This book takes an in-depth look into conflict resolution. Most conflict resolution books look at addressing conflict in the workplace, but few discuss the conflict we face in our everyday lives. Disarming conflict is a critical aspect of violence prevention, but just one of many. My business SAFE International has taught over 250,000 people how to recognize, avoid, or deal with conflict and violence. We are a world leader in teaching practical, effective, and memorable life-saving content.

If you would like to take a deep dive into the world of violence prevention for yourself or your loved ones.

Don't Wait!

Sign up to our latest website at **www.safe101.education** to receive lots of free tips, videos, and other valuable life-saving resources.

DEDICATIONS

My Family

One can't spend twenty-five years launching, building, and sustaining a business in violence prevention without support from so many people. This begins with my family: foremost my wife, Sherry, and my grown children, Shane and Devyn, who have allowed and supported me to follow this dream despite the crazy hours, travel, and day-to-day requirements to do so. And my sister, Karen, who has always been there with the honesty and support I have often needed and my parents who are no longer with us but always supported me from the day I suggested the idea of beginning this business. Today, my biggest inspiration is my two granddaughters, Kinsley and Jade, who are always in my thoughts in every project I take on. I dedicate this book to all of you with my love!

BOOK FOREWORD

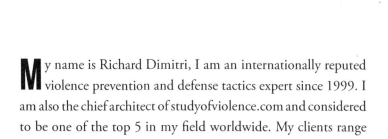

My name is Richard Dimitri, I am an internationally reputed violence prevention and defense tactics expert since 1999. I am also the chief architect of studyofviolence.com and considered to be one of the top 5 in my field worldwide. My clients range from high schools to the Finnish Presidential Security Team and everyone in between. Having taught in 22 countries and met most of the experts in our field, finding one who cared more about their clients than their tough-guy images, personal bank accounts and reputations was like trying to find a contact lens in a swimming pool.

In 2010, one of these experts contacted me while I was in Cairo, Egypt working with several international women's movements, his name is Chris Roberts, the founder of SAFE International and the author of this book. Chris contacted me to learn more about a specific concept I had originated and to set a workshop up with him in the greater Toronto area.

We became fast friends and eventually, best of, which is why he asked me to write this foreword. The reason we connected so well was that we shared the same dreams and goals regarding our work in the violence prevention and self-defense industry, and that is to reduce senseless violence worldwide and by proxy, strengthening communities and relationships. Chris is one of the rare few who cares more about people than he does his image and rep. The man tirelessly works at improving himself and the information he shares with the public.

When Chris decided to teach self-defense full time and from scratch open a business to do so, he was part owner of a successful fast-food chain that would have guaranteed him a secure and more than comfortable income, but he quit it all to follow his heart and passion.

In 1994, Chris started SAFE International, and today, he works with over 80 high schools across eastern Canada, as well as First Nations, health care centers, corporations and all those in need of pure and applied self-defense. His work has saved too many lives to innumerate here, and even though he suffers from a rare neurological dysfunction that has literally taken his voice from him, nothing could shut this man's passion and drive to help people out. Not only did he not quit as most would have in his shoes, he instead turned his disability into rocket-fueled motivation to grow his legacy project and certify people worldwide to spread his message of peace through violence prevention.

This is what makes him perfect for writing this book. The information he shares is scientifically sound, well researched and filled with personal experiences from countless victims of every kind of abuse and violence one can think of which Chris helped get through via his work.

This book is for anyone, and everyone, not just for the prevention of violence as the information contained transcends to any and all types of conflicts, including personal relationships, but to improve on communication skills as well as establishing a greater understanding of human behaviour concerning conflict and violence.

Thank you, I hope you enjoy it as much as I did.

Sincerely,
Richard Dimitri

CONTENTS

INTRODUCTION

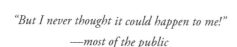

"But I never thought it could happen to me!"
—most of the public

I n today's frenzied world, we notice or face conflict daily with our loved ones, coworkers, or strangers in the street. Conflict often ends with both people chuckling over the silliness of the issue, coming to a joint resolution, or agreeing to disagree. Still, more and more often, we open up our computer or turn on the news to discover a story where someone has *died*—yes, *died*— or received a severe injury, which may range from a concussion to a coma, as the result of a conflict. When you're not directly involved, these matters usually involve something seemingly trivial or insignificant. And the scary part is virtually no one thinks something like that could ever happen to them, yet it does happen. You might be watching a video of a conflict that grabs your attention. You see CCTV footage capturing in graphic detail someone knocking someone out with a right hook to the jaw. Their body goes limp, their head smacks the ground, their body is still, no movement at all, so you assume that the guilty party must be a thug. Sadly, your assumptions may be wrong at first glance. Good people, in fact, some usually amazingly kind, thoughtful people are finding themselves in front of a judge or, worse, dead because they made one poor decision in a moment of conflict. We have all made poor decisions in conflict, and luckily no one gets hurt most of the time, but it does happen—and much more often than you might think or want to believe.

So, who is this book for?

Have you ever faced conflict and said the first words that came to your mind without hesitation only to find the situation getting worse? Then this book is for you.

Have you ever automatically taken a defensive position with someone before even understanding what the issue might be? Then this book is for you.

Have you ever had someone react to you in conflict with words or body language that raised your blood pressure and heart rate and made you clench your fists or want to smack them? Then this book is for you.

Would you like to provide your kids with strategies on how to deal with conflict? This book is for you.

Do you have a loved one, friend, or coworker who flies off the handle instantly when confronted? Does this cause you to worry about their safety? Then this book is for them—but also you so you can show them the negative potential outcomes of their actions.

This book will provide you with practical tools and strategies to understand, recognize, and handle all types of conflict. It will offer you real-life education, not unproven content that has only been applied in a classroom setting. This book will increase your chances of getting home to who and what really matters.... your *loved ones*!

Countless people who have participated in our violence prevention programs have expressed, often with deep emotion, how they now think of conflict and violence with a completely different paradigm. Prior to the program, they never understood the role they played in the conflict and how close they came to lose all that is truly important in their lives.

My *promise* to you is that if you adopt these strategies, you will enter all conflicts with new confidence. You will dramatically reduce the chances of escalating conflict or the chances of violence, and you will have the ability to de-escalate conflict, resulting in a win-win-win scenario! A win for you, a win for the person you're in conflict with, and a win for those you love because you got back to them safely. Ultimate success is when no one gets hurt, the police aren't required, and no one is standing in front of a judge having to explain their actions. But for many, all those things do happen even when they didn't need to.

Do not be the type of person who thinks, "Okay, I know it happens, but it will never happen to me!" Ask anyone with firsthand experience with conflict that has gotten out of control or lost a family member to it. They will tell you they wish they had known and understood the tools to manage conflict. Or ask anyone who has faced the court system, spent time in jail, or hurt someone else because they didn't understand conflict, violence, and their role in it; they will tell you they wish they had followed the principles and concepts you will read in this book.

So, let's dive into the compelling world of conflict resolution!

CHAPTER 1

WHAT IS CONFLICT?

I can handle myself... I thought!

It was around 1982 or 1983, I was living near Cornwall, Ontario, a border city with Massena, New York. Often on weekends, we would cross the border and go to one of the many Massena bars. One night I was with six or seven friends at a bar that had an upstairs with tables where you could have a drink while watching the dance floor below. A few of us were upstairs drinking, having a few laughs when one of my friends accidentally knocked into his drink with his arm. The glass toppled over the bannister, landing near or hitting a woman, I can't recall exactly. But what I do remember vividly is a large group of guys, within what seemed like seconds, surrounding our table on the upper level with words and facial expressions that revealed a strong desire to kill us. Names were being hurled back and forth, and none of those names were very endearing.

We tried to explain it was an accident, but no one wanted to hear our honest explanation. Our apologies turned to anger, but we were greatly outnumbered. Luckily, the club bouncers arrived before it got beyond a few shoves back and forth. The security staff told us to get out of the bar and go back to Canada, and they would give us about five minutes of lead time. So, we took it! I'm pretty sure that, being young, stupid, and full of ego, we discussed in the car how lucky those guys were that the bouncers had shown up and saved them, not us. But if you were able to read our minds, I would bet each of us was counting our lucky stars we were safe, we thought, in our vehicles heading back to Cornwall. Think the story is over? Not at all.

We headed to the Fat Albert's Sandwich shop, which was our standard practice after a night out drinking. We were laughing about what had happened when guess who entered the shop? Two or three of the guys who had confronted us at the bar. Damn, they were Canadians! Well, that did not matter to me anyway. I proceeded to stand up, point and yell across the busy restaurant something to the effect of, "Hey, there are the stupid assholes from the bar." One guy instantly yelled back, "Why don't you say that to my face, buddy?" At the time, I thought this was an excellent opportunity to show my physical abilities if need be, since no bouncers were present to separate us. The ironic part is that I had no skills to defend myself at the time, but somehow my ego told me I did. And with the added fact that I had been drinking, the rational part of my brain was not functioning at 100 percent.

Maybe, in the back of my mind, I was hoping someone would intervene so I could act tough, impress my friends, and then have a story to share. Well, it's true that I was developing a story to share, but not the one I saw in my mind. So, I got up close, chest to chest with this guy. I looked up at him and thought, Wow, he's a lot bigger when you get close to him. He said, "So, I am an asshole, eh? How about you give the reasons why?" I took that as a legitimate question, so I proceeded to answer him, offering options A, B, and somewhere around option C, something hit me swiftly, directly, and right on target with my jaw. It was his elbow, beautifully placed. Well, I assume it was ideally placed since I don't remember much after that, except a vague recollection of people jumping to their defense, not ours. Since there were more of us than them, they automatically assumed we were the "bad guys."

Even after tasting what an elbow to my jaw felt like, I'm not sure I really learned any lessons other than that I'm not particularly eager to get hit. It was only years later when I began my journey into the world of self-defense and violence prevention that I understood what had happened and that I had gone against everything I teach today. Honestly, I haven't faced a lot of violence in my life, but with what experiences I have encountered and heard from others, I now understand how close any confrontation can come to life-altering results. This book will be a mixture of stories from my own experiences, what I have seen and read online, and stories people have shared with me.

Throughout the book, you'll hear me use the terms conflict, confrontation, and violence. Conflict and confrontation have some similarities, but a few differences. For example, if you find yourself in a confrontation, you may be standing in front of a single person or a group of people. It may be a serious disagreement or something trivial. From there, conflict is often the next stage where your words and body language are escalating, teetering on violence. Then you have violence, which is the physical act where harming, assaulting, raping, or killing someone is intended by one or both parties. Now, violence may not have been the intention at the beginning for either party, but the buildup, the threatening manner, the words, and their tone along with the egos involved might result in a split-second decision to use violence, whether in a controlled thought-out manner or through a lack of control.

It is essential to understand that some confrontation may start off at a very superficial level but can reach perilous heights in a flash. Self-defense companies generally put their focus on the violence segment, which is essential, but if that's all they focus on, then, in my opinion, they are irresponsible. If one is genuinely teaching real violence prevention, you don't want to get to that stage of the conflict. If violence prevention or self-defense is the alphabet, to begin at the physical techniques or moves is like starting at the letter M. It does not make sense, but it's how many sell their "system" or "style." We're going to put the focus on beginning at the letter A. Understanding both confrontation and conflict, recognizing them, and learning how to control and manage ourselves so we can address them with the ultimate outcome of having no harm come to ourselves or anyone else involved.

And then, if all that fails, one needs to understand how to use violence as a tool responsibly, morally, and ethically to achieve the same outcome of getting home to who and what matters.

I might point out that I'm not a fan of the term "self-defense." But there is a critical word in it that is perfectly suited to conflict resolution. That is the word "self." We can't begin to address conflict without taking a hard, honest look in the mirror at ourselves. How do we see ourselves reacting in conflict? How have we responded in the past? Can you think of a time when you came face to face with someone in any scenario where circumstances brought you together and either you accused them of some wrongdoing or they got in your face, hurling accusations at you?

Perhaps it was a case of road rage, or someone bumping into you or accusing you of something you did or did not do. Can you remember the emotions? Can you feel your ego kicking in and telling you something like, "You aren't going to take that from them, are you?" or "How dare they speak to you like that!" Sit with that feeling for a moment.

> "If you face just one opponent and you doubt yourself,
> you're outnumbered."—Dan Millman

Regardless of which side of the conflict you were on, how clearheaded were you? Were you scared, angry, out of control of your emotions? What were the first words that came to your mind and even worse, did you say them? How did you express those words? How did they react to those words? I'm going to guess they didn't back down and humbly agree with you, did they?

Most people think conflict management begins here, but they would be incorrect. It starts with you, your beliefs, your life experiences, how you were raised, and how you were taught. Perhaps you had a parent who told you that you must stand up for yourself in all situations; you don't take shit from anyone. Or maybe you saw others around you supposedly getting ahead in life by dominating people and conversations through aggression or manipulation? Some get ahead by using conflict negatively through bullying others to get what they want in their work-life and at home. Maybe it has worked for you to this stage in your life, or you *think* it has worked.

But then one day, you may find yourself in the middle of what appears and feels to be a typical conflict you've experienced a hundred times before with someone you've never met. Perhaps they're staring directly into your eyes with a menacing look while screaming at you and accusing you of something. But you think, No big deal. I'll respond the way I always do, by getting in their face, raising my voice, and presenting threatening body language and attitude. They'll be intimidated by me and back down like everyone else has. You may even be chuckling to yourself because it's a game for you. You puff out your chest, get louder than they are, and take a few steps closer in that threatening manner you've perfected.

But this time, the person doesn't even flinch or show the tiniest bit of fear. In fact, they laugh at you, and bystanders see them laughing, making you the focal point and joke of the conflict. Everyone is now staring at you; out of reflex, you might even jump to the standard male line of "What's your fuckin' problem" to which they respond, "What's my problem? You are!" which they express with a confidence that is foreign to you. Rather than backing down, they get even more heated because you've now challenged them with your words, tone of voice, and body language. At this point, both parties are heavily engaged in the "fight"—the fight to be right, the battle to not lose face, the struggle to teach the other person a lesson.

The example I just shared with you is very typical. Neither person dares to take a step back, afraid to show a sign of weakness. And frequently, there may be shoves back and forth until someone intervenes and breaks up the altercation. But another common scenario occurs when one person launches a punch like they've done multiple times in these seemingly minor conflicts. Your strike lands on the intended target, and the other person goes down like a sack of potatoes, bam! You look around with a smile on your face, but when you turn back to admire your work, you observe the other person isn't even moving. You nervously laugh it off for a moment but see the blood coming out of the side of their head, trickling down their cheek because you knocked them unconscious when you punched them. So, they were at the mercy of whatever their head landed on when they fell. Your perfect punch knocked them out before they even hit the pavement, so they didn't have time to brace themselves. And I will add that even that first simple shove could have resulted in the same outcome.

Then the panic sets in and your mind is scrambling, going through a Rolodex of options. You might think to run if no one is around. Or you may jump in to help the person because it was a stupid fight or argument, and you never meant to seriously hurt them or kill them, but you have. You might run through all the outcomes in your head. Best-case scenario, they have a severe concussion, but then you think, what if I put them in a coma? At this point, your whole life may flash before your eyes, and you may panic. In an instant, you may have not only killed someone but destroyed multiple lives, including your own. In a flash, you may have taken someone's father, brother, sister, spouse, or best friend away from them. You think of your own family and how they will be crushed and destroyed. In that flash of bravado, machismo, you thought you just wanted to teach them a lesson or show them they can't talk to you like that. Why did they not just back down? You may wonder why they did not back down, still blaming them for their actions, but guess how the law is going to see it? See the law doesn't care who started the fight, what it was over, who was right or wrong—just what happened, the result was, and what your part in it was.

At this moment, many conflicts are playing out like this somewhere in the world. Far too often, this senseless, unnecessary infantile violence plays out with neither party ever imagining it will end with disastrous results.

How many different decisions would we make in our lives if we could see even just a couple seconds into the future? Futures get devastated in a momentary lapse of rational thinking because we never anticipate what might go wrong when we're heavily invested in our egos and resolute in proving someone else wrong regardless of the reasons behind any conflict.

This is where the term violence comes in. It is the extension of a conflict but may also be the initial intention of the dispute by one of the parties involved.

Let's stop here for a moment because this is critical. It is interesting how often conflict ends with one person backing down, tail between their legs, and a quick exit out of the location to save face and many perceive that person as being weak.

But they're alive and may not realize what catastrophe they just avoided for either of them. But often no one backs down, both are rage-filled. One or both will lose control and purposely throw a punch, pull a weapon, or grab, maybe shove, the other person to the ground. They might jump on them and begin pounding the crap out of the person. Then they get up, look around and celebrate their victory! Sure, someone gets hurt, but no big deal, right? They'll heal up and lick their wounds, and the "winner" can brag to their friends.

And do not mistake stories like this to only have male involvement. They happen between males, females, or both. You may think it generally happens between males, but confrontation, conflict, and violence have no gender.

Here are two examples. The first story took place in British Columbia, Canada.

> *Lawrence Sharp, 42, who was found guilty of manslaughter assaulted Michael Page-Vincelli who died from injuries he sustained after being punched unconscious, falling and hitting his head at a Starbucks in Burnaby on July 12, 2017.* [1]

> *Court heard Page-Vincelli, 22, was likely knocked out instantly. He fell and hit his head on the floor hard enough to cause a fracture to his skull and bleeding around his brain. He was declared brain dead the following day and died on July 15, 2017.* [2]

This is a horrific story but incidents like this are becoming more common in society. I do not know either person. Most people will assume that the person who knocked out the other guy must be a criminal, a thug, "bad guy." Most of the time, though, a situation like this involves an average guy at the

1   https://www.cbc.ca/news/canada/british-columbia/michael-page-vincelli-death-sucker-punch-lawrence-sharpe-sentencing-1.5268680

2   https://www.birminghammail.co.uk/news/midlands-news/deers-leap-single-punch-killed-7436318

mercy of his emotions, making the worst possible decision, not knowing or expecting the result of killing another human being and being sentenced to jail.

This second example was shared with me by my friend and violence prevention instructor Darren Norton in the UK.

What also makes this story even more tragic is that the gentleman who died from a single punch was a dad of one and was trying to break up a fight; he wasn't the one instigating it.

Obviously, these examples are worst-case scenarios, but I like to address worst-case because, if we can understand them and the repercussions, we're much more likely to respect conflict and the potential for harm from the earliest point.

Read on for strategies to help make sure you never find yourself in front of a judge, waiting to hear your sentence or have your family come to the morgue to identify your body.

CONFLICT CONTEMPLATION

- Think of conflicts you've faced over your life. Have you considered what the repercussions of your actions could have been?
- Do you regularly face conflicts?

CHAPTER 2

TYPES OF CONFLICT

*"Conflict is drama, and how people deal with conflict
shows you the kind of people they are."*
—Stephen Moyer

onflict falls under two primary categories: circumstantial events or purposeful targeting. There's a big difference between the two, and one has much more significant potential for violence. Understanding each will help you understand and establish the optimal strategies for finding a resolution or preparation for action.

Because conflict often happens so quickly, we need to establish as fast as possible what and who we're potentially dealing with. As my friend and fellow violence prevention expert Richard Dimitri likes to say, "Are we dealing with a good guy having a bad day or a *bad guy*?"[3]

---

3   I use the term "guy" to mean either male or female.

CIRCUMSTANTIAL CONFLICT

With circumstantial conflict, you may be going about your day like any other day. You could be headed to work, at work, in a grocery store, at a sporting event, in your home, or on vacation. In a moment, you find yourself in a scenario with someone else due to circumstances no one planned. You may have an issue with the other person or they with you. This could play out in countless scenarios. Just a few may include, but are not limited to:

1) The other person feels you've wronged them somehow. Perhaps it was something they heard or were told about you, and they are now confronting you.
2) You've cut them off in traffic or bumped into them unknowingly in a line.
3) The person thinks you were looking disrespectfully at their significant other at the bar.
4) You took their parking spot.
5) You gave them a look that was challenging.
6) They believe your child banged your shopping cart into their car in the parking lot.
7) An argument over a sports team.

Any scenario that you never anticipated or planned might fall under the category of circumstantial.

PURPOSEFUL TARGETING

In the case of purposeful targeting, it is generally much more dangerous. Where circumstantial conflict is not preplanned, in this case, one of the parties has purposely chosen someone as a victim. Their choice of a victim may fall under one of the following wants or desires on their part:

1) Sexual assault
2) Physical assault
3) Murder
4) Bullying—many make the mistake of thinking bullying does not fit in with the likes of the other three types, but there is an intended target and harm may quickly come in all four situations.

The challenge in this type of conflict is that the perpetrator already has a general or detailed plan. They've already one or multiple steps ahead of their intended target—chosen for victimization—and the idea may have been in the works for just a few minutes or over an extended period.

With purposeful targeting, it will be challenging to verbally de-escalate the aggressor and to convince them not to follow through with their intentions since they chose their victim with intention and based on several criteria.

Fortunately, learning certain strategies will set you up for the best chance of success, regardless of whether you've been targeted, or the conflict is circumstantial.

CIRCUMSTANTIAL MOVES TO TARGETED

There is also another variation, one that begins as circumstantial but becomes targeted.

You may find yourself in a circumstantial scenario with a very high probability you can verbally de-escalate the other person. Still, through your or their body language, words, and tone, it escalates to the point where one of you decides to cause harm to the other. Most people have no idea now that they are increasing conflict when they could quickly defuse it with some simple strategies. You may genuinely think you are de-escalating the other person when, in fact, you're doing the opposite.

Regardless of which type of conflict you face, there are high stake risks if one isn't educated on how to handle it.

THE GOAL IN CONFLICT—WIN-WIN-WIN

Many approach conflicts with the attitude that to win, the other person must lose. With a view like that from the outset, it is harder to resolve the conflict using the effective strategies given in this book.

Therefore, it's imperative to understand what you might lose if a conflict goes wrong. And when I say lose, I don't mean losing face, pride, or reputation. The fear of losing what matters most in your life should be paramount and top of mind if you find yourself in any conflict, whether seemingly small or significant. Consider what you may lose.

- You may lose your freedom.
- You may lose your finances.

- You may lose your life.
- You may lose your family.

And in turn, the other person may lose those same precious things as well.

The goal should always be to avoid conflict, so you win, the other person wins, and by default, those who matter to you win, too.

CONFLICT CONTEMPLATION

- What types of conflict have you faced?
- Are you able to recognize which type it was?
- Do you recall having the goal to de-escalate it?

CHAPTER 3

COMMUNICATION IN CONFLICT

"Respectful communication under conflict or opposition is
an essential and truly awe-inspiring ability."
—Bryant McGill, *Voice of Reason*

When people hear the word communication, they usually think the words they use are the backbone when, in fact, words are just *one* of the ways people communicate with others. In fact, they may even be the least important aspect of body language.

When you see someone in a rage, out of control, and yelling, it is their body language that is prominent in sending you communication, followed by the tone of the words, and last, the actual words.

Lots of statistics claim that body language accounts for up to 90 percent of communication. According to Psychology Today, communication generally breaks down this way: 55 percent is body language, 38 percent is tone of voice, and 7 percent is the actual words spoken.[4] Remember, everyone is different and scenarios vary, but you can see a framework here that the vast majority of people will fit into, and these statistics give you an idea of how little the actual words matter when compared to the body language and tone.

In most conflicts, if your goal is to avoid harm, it's usually not smart to verbalize the first thoughts that come to mind. Those thoughts are influenced by your mental state, which is being fueled by adrenalin and anxiety at that point. Now, if your goal is to *begin* a fight, those first words may undoubtedly help. But, before you utter them, it is important to understand all the consequences they may hold.

BODY LANGUAGE CUES

Let's focus first on body language. It's critical to understand that the person you're communicating with sends you messages through their body language. Once you understand those messages, it will help you decipher the different signals. From there, you can establish your strategy. Again, what makes it challenging is the physical and mental state you'll be in, depending on the severity of the issue at the time. You may not be thinking clearly, which is why educating yourself on body language is crucial in the hopes of picking up on the cues more effectively.

Another complicating factor is that more than one message is being sent to you at a time, which adds to the confusion.

---

4   https://www.psychologytoday.com/ca/blog/beyond-words/201109/is-nonverbal-communication-numbers-game

It is important not to get tunnel vision and only see one cue. Keep in mind that you also could be getting mixed messages, which may or may not be intentional on the other person's part. Those messages could be used to set you up for violence—or you could be misreading them. You may have just a second or just a few minutes to react in any conflict, so the ability to read body language as early as possible is critical.

Imagine you're in a restaurant. You look out the window and see someone hurrying to their car because they know the city parking enforcement officer is writing a ticket. The person appears to be shouting with their hands erratically flailing in the air while they're running to the car. Their face has a look of frustration on it, and their body movements are getting bigger. As they get closer to the law enforcement officer, the officer takes a few steps back and puts their hands up, not aggressively but in a controlled passive manner, appearing to be in fear. Without hearing a single word, the body language of both people gives you a pretty strong message or sense of what is going on. You can't listen to the people, but can you imagine the language and words being used. The body language is going to be prominent in how you interpret the event.

On the contrary, if you only read the words being said on paper without being able to see the emotion and gestures behind them, they would not have nearly the same impact on you, would they?

Why do I mention this? Because as a witness or uninvolved bystander, it's much easier to pick up on the messages the body language sends from all involved, but when you are one of the people in the scene, you may miss many of the cues if you're not aware of them or what to look for.

SESAME STREET ANALOGY

You may hear the words and their tone and get one message, and then see the body language, which may or may not match what you're hearing. Remember the Sesame Street game where they sang, "One of these things is not like the others. One of these things doesn't belong."[5]

That is an excellent analogy to bring into conflict resolution. For example, picture this guy with that angered expression on his face and his hands up aggressively. If he was standing inches from you but saying, "I don't want any trouble!" you would have to agree that there is a vast discrepancy between what he is saying and what his body language is telling you. You would see the body language first, before you took in the words.

---

5   https://www.youtube.com/watch?v=rsRjQDrDnY8

Here are a few more examples of different body language. Look at each one and ask yourself what would immediately come to mind if they presented themselves to you. Don't worry about any scenario or conflict, look at them and ask yourself, "If I didn't hear any words, what would I think they were telling me in this picture?" You might see things like:

- They are telling me they're angry.
- They appear frustrated.
- They look very sad.
- They look disappointed.
- They're telling me they're about to hit me.
- They look apologetic, like they're guilty.

The more details you can notice, the better, but once again, it's very different when you're sitting calmly with time to analyze each picture. The interaction will be happening quickly, possibly with just a few seconds or less to identify what the body language is telling you.

Some of the pictures will send a powerful, unmistakable message to you where others may be more subtle or have more than one possible meaning. The more we can familiarize ourselves with the different faces and possible messages, the more options we'll have when the conflict comes.

For example, you might immediately think someone looks frustrated, but someone else looking at the same picture might say, "They don't look frustrated. They look pissed!" There are subtle nuances that can be essential to pick up on and what looks one way to one person may look very different to someone else. If you thought a person looked frustrated, when in fact, they were angry, your reaction might be different between the two. There are no guarantees, and no one is perfect at picking up all the exact cues, but with practice, you can increase your chances of getting them correct.

Here is a simple game you can play. Whenever you're out, make "people watching" a game. Look at someone and see how quickly you can come up with a strong thought on how you think they feel/what their emotions are at any given moment. But be open-minded enough to question yourself. You may be surprised how quickly you jump to conclusions.

Then watch two people in a discussion and aim to establish what you believe the conversation might be about. Is it friendly, cold, in mild disagreement over something, or is one person upset with the other? Do it from a safe distance where you only have the body language to go by. It is truly fascinating what you'll see if you're looking for it.

When you can hear the dialogue with a specific tone to it, that adds valuable input to what you're already receiving from the body language. As noted previously, the context of the scenario adds to the body language, words, and tone. For example, if you see a person with a look on their face in an office because they just got reprimanded for poor job performance, you may think its frustration and worry that they will lose their job. Still, if you witness this same look on a stranger who has had a few drinks, and you are in a bar beside them and heard that they just got off the phone with their girlfriend who you establish has just broken up with them, you might get a substantially different message. So, when viewing the same look on the face in a different context coupled with the words and tone, you might come to a very different conclusion.

By searching for all these cues when you're calm, you'll be able to slowly adapt it to conversations you're in, whether they're just a friendly conversation or an actual conflict. As a bonus to searching for these cues in your own discussions, you will appear to really be listening to the other person. So not only is it a beautiful thing to do but it is also strategic.

People give apparent cues of anger, frustration, fear, anxiety, and aggression when they're standing in front of another person. And behind those cues, they may give much more subtle ones, which will be very challenging to pick up when engaged in any heated conflict. They are often referred to as micro expressions. Have you ever watched the television show *Lie to Me* with Tim Roth? It is based on using micro expressions to determine whether someone is lying. It's a fascinating show when you watch it to educate yourself on even more subtleties.

Another cue on top of the more obvious ones may include the gritting of one's teeth. That may be a strong indication that the person is enraged, likely building in aggression to either intimidate you or building up to hitting you.

If you take the gritting of the teeth and see them shuffling side to side in an almost bouncing fashion or making erratic movements, those together are another powerful indication they're getting ready to hit you.

If you witness gritting of teeth, shuffling side to side, and then you see them angle off with one-hand opening and closing or just closed, that's an even stronger indication they're about to hit you.

Then if you take the gritting of the teeth, the shuffling, the angling off with a hand making a fist, and they begin looking around, then they're looking to see if there may be witnesses or attempting to distract you before they strike you.

If they're not in range to hit you, you may also see them moving closer to you. (That is a critical issue we will discuss in the next chapter.)

You can see many cues to what is about to happen, but if you're not aware of them, you could easily get caught up in your emotion and ego and not even notice what is quite apparent.

It's adrenalin and tunnel vision in a severe conflict that causes people to be blind to what is in front of them, where if they were watching a movie with the same details, they would yell at the screen, "Hey, Buddy, he is about to punch you!"

The important difference is that in one scenario, you're on a couch eating popcorn and having a beer with no adrenalin rush, fear, or anxiety. In the other scenario, you're in the moment, crapping your pants and oblivious to the cues.

Unless you've read a book like this or taken any of our violence prevention/self-defense courses. Watch this video, and you'll see some of the cues I mentioned.[6]

What did you see? Would you have noticed all those cues without even the simple precontact cues I just offered? Precontact cues signal what is possibly coming, and when you stack them

---

6   https://www.youtube.com/watch?v=FRicVkpCKsE

on top of each other, you get a more accurate picture. Here lies the challenge: How do you do all this in the moment of conflict, particularly if it is heated?

To add to the complication, if you've never met the person before, you can mix up the cues. You might see someone in a nonthreatening scenario and think they look aggressive or angry even when they're in a neutral state, but that might be their natural body language or appearance.

Anyone you face whom you have not met is unknown to you. You have no idea of the person's history, typical demeanor, or everyday language, so to say that these cues mentioned are the exact same for everyone would be inaccurate.

But in conflict, if you listen and use the right words in the proper tone, you can nudge them into giving you accurate clues, all the while not escalating them. And if the tension does increase even after using all the possible principles and concepts I'm offering, that is a clue that you need to prepare yourself physically if you can't escape or exit.

TONE & WORDS

I mentioned that the tone of the words is the second most crucial part of communication. People think that if someone is angry, they'll yell, but there are also differences within the sound of their voice. Someone may be yelling, screaming, and approaching you quickly, whereas someone else's anger or aggression may be displayed with a shallow, slowed down tone along with a menacing slow approach toward you.

As I've taught for twenty-five years, there are no definite answers in any scenario, and if you make the mistake of thinking conflict will always look the same from one person to another, you could be in danger. Even with your own circle of family and friends, do you not see a vast array of subtleties in how people display emotions and use their words?

It's important to understand the *feelings* and *intuition* you get from behind the words people are using. Fear is a good example. When people are fearful, their voice and tone may show it. Their voice may sound shaky or hoarse or have pitch changes due to the anxiety and stress of the moment. It may crack or one might even lose their voice momentarily. Sometimes no words will come out if they freeze in the moment. Other times the words may not make sense as their mind is scrambling to find suitable ones. And for others, the words come flying out, but most often not in an effective way. Exhibiting fear in conflict is entirely reasonable. Anyone who says they don't fear anything is lying. Even those experienced in dealing with violence will tell you they experience fear; they just manage it better. And your display of fear can be an advantage if a scenario is moving toward an actual physical attack, but more on that later. Interestingly, people often think their fear stems from the words the other person says, when, in fact, it's the body language and tone that's really causing them fear.

Speaking of words used in conflict, it is essential to mention the use of foul language. Some people use foul language as part of their day-to-day speech while others rarely, if ever, swear. From experience, those who are not comfortable with foul language are the ones who most often react negatively when they hear it, mainly if it is directed at them in anger.

While some use profanity for no other reason than it is their style, some use it for the purpose of eliciting a response or to cripple the person they're directing the words at.

My business, SAFE International, has taught more than 200,000 high school teens. We usually ask the teachers if we can use "foul language" in our demos. We promise to use it in the context of a scenario the students may face. And by the way, this is pertinent to all ages, but I want to make a point with my high school teen example. Now, to emphasize, again I'm not saying we want to teach a whole class with f-bombs flying all over the place. That is unnecessary and not professional in some settings, but it is critical to understand that not using it or addressing it in teaching is a massive disservice to our clients when we know foul language is a part of conflict.

Road rage situations are classic examples of when profanity may be prevalent. And road rage scenarios are becoming more and more common, so they are given their own chapter further on. For now, though, let's look at a simple case of someone seeing you from a distance and they mistake your glance at them for staring. They cross the road at a fast, aggressive pace and say something like, "What the fuck are you looking at, *asshole*?"

Now immediately you might get your back up and say the typical phrase, "I wasn't looking at you. What's your problem anyway?" Now typically from that, the next step is the primitive chest-thumping verbal exchange of "I don't have a problem, but you do now!" Back and forth it goes, and things escalate.

Now, the initial question of "What the fuck you are looking at, *asshole*" could be merely a reflex response from someone who's having a bad day. They might typically never respond like that but remember the importance of context. What if they just lost their job? Or their wife or husband just dumped them, and their ex told them they will not see their kids again? So, with the culmination of their day, maybe they'd just had more than they can take. They saw you and totally misread your glance. It is not personal, but they're at the mercy of their emotions, as we all are, whether we're highly trained in violence prevention or not. Immediately getting defensive with them while they're in that heightened state of feeling is a recipe for disaster whether they or you know it. Be cautious. You don't know the person in front of you, their history, or what they're capable of.

Or take this same example, and the person is walking around looking for conflict, looking for a vulnerable target. They may say again, "What the fuck are you looking at, *asshole?*" But this time, they're looking for your reaction and perhaps any excuse to engage in a fight. Your response will be critical. Again, there are no definite answers, but if you meet them with that defensiveness again, they may think, Great, I have my excuse to beat the crap out of this person. As twisted as it may seem, there are many looking for conflict. They may just be having a bad day and can't control their emotions now, and you've presented yourself as a relief for their anxiety. Or they may just enjoy it.

What I'm pointing out is that in one case, the words a person uses may be out of a lack of control and due to their emotions at the time, but they may also be a tool to find a potential target. You do not know the other person's intentions, so you need to understand that while you can't control their behavior, you can control yours if you have insights on the topic of conflict.

Don't forget how hard it can be to stay in control when you're in a hostile moment.

Remember, words are just words! Someone may use specific words in order to have power over you if you let them, but if you understand this, you can better strategize.

An extreme example, and one I will go into in a separate chapter, is in a sexual assault scenario. If a male rapist has cornered a woman in an isolated location, and he has violently grabbed her ponytail, snapping her neck back, and leaned in close to the woman's face, focusing on the fear in her eyes while controlling her head and describing in horrific detail what he is going to do to her, she will be terrified. Still, if she lets those details and words cripple her, then the rapist has used them effectively to accomplish what he wants. He wants compliance and often will get that by using extreme language and domination. Do you see how that is very effective for the rapist?

But if she remembers that those are just words and that they're being used to attempt to shut her down, then she can use them to her advantage due to several psychological strategies.

CONFLICT CONTEMPLATION

- Do you recall a conflict and the body language of the other person?
- Were they confrontational, neutral, or fearful?
- What was your body language in the conflict?
- Did your words and tone match your body language?
- What was your goal in the conflict?

CHAPTER 4

YOU FIND YOURSELF IN A CONFLICT

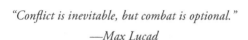

"Conflict is inevitable, but combat is optional."
—Max Lucad

So, there you are going about your day and a conflict happens. I haven't given you any incident at this point. We'll cover a few specific scenarios in a bit, but I want to offer some general tips and advice that are relevant regardless of the conflict.

CONTEXT OF SCENARIO

Where is this taking place? Is it taking place in your home, in the workplace, in a bar, or on public transportation? Perhaps you're in a parking lot of a grocery store or a tourist in a foreign country. Your environment can play a massive part in any conflict. Being familiar with the location can be an asset or a detriment depending on who is involved. If you're in a foreign country, unfamiliar with the surroundings, that can have some disadvantages if you have no idea where to run or where the police might be located. Maybe you're in a hockey arena surrounded by concrete, which might play a role if you were to be knocked to the ground.

If you can exit the scene safely before it gets confrontational, do so. Now when I say exit, I don't mean like a hit and run. Perhaps the environment you're in is unsafe, and you would be better to continue it in a public setting. You could be in your car on the side of the road, when it's dark outside, with vehicles whizzing past, which creates the potential for harm. Put your four-way flashers on, drive the speed limit, and go somewhere less hazardous.

Can you return inside the store to a safer spot where other staff or management might be if someone is confronting you in a dark or isolated parking lot?

If you're using public transportation, can you move toward the driver near the front where you may be safer?

I also like to get somewhere more public since so many people have cell phones these days, and there's an excellent chance someone will begin filming if they hear raised voices. Currently, people are more likely to pull out their cellphone and film you than come to your assistance. Having a video of the conflict can help you if it goes beyond a mild confrontation, and you end up in court. Also, CCTV cameras are everywhere these days, which can work to your advantage or against it. Now, I'm not saying cameras will prevent conflict since people will assault someone or rob a convenience store fully aware, they're being filmed. Often, they don't care, or their emotions get the better of them and they can't process that their actions are being recorded.

How many people are involved directly or indirectly? If you're in a one-on-one scenario, that will be much different than a conflict where the person has three friends with them. What happens if you have your kids, spouse, or someone else with you? All these questions come into play, not only from the perspective of you not wanting a loved one to be harmed but also because you don't know how they might react. Your loved one might inadvertently escalate the scenario.

Could there be weapons? The other person may have weapons, but you haven't seen them yet. At SAFE International™ we teach that in any conflict, you should assume the other person does have something that can be used as a weapon.

The weather also might play a factor. Are you in conflict on a sidewalk and ice or rain has made the surface very slippery?

What is the other person's or your state of mind or health at the time? Do you have the flu and can barely function when you find yourself in conflict? Did the other person receive some devastating news that is affecting their emotions? Are you in a bar where you may or may not have been drinking? Has the other person been drinking? If either of you suffer from any mental illness, that may also contribute.

All these factors are going to influence the conflict for better or worse. Some you may have some control over, but many you will not. Just understand that it is rare for anyone to be 100 percent on top of their mental and emotional game.

MENTAL ILLNESS

Another factor that plays in the context of the situation is whether the person has a mental illness. Bringing up mental illness was once a taboo subject but now more people will discuss it. I will state upfront I'm no authority on the topic. I have no academic training to deal with mental illness but feel it necessary to bring up the topic in a book on conflict since it is so prevalent. In fact, according to the World Health Organization, mental or neurological disorders will affect one in four people in their life. So why do I bring this up? Again, it goes to my statement about not knowing who the person in front of you might be or what their health history is. The strategies in this book are valuable, whether you know of a mental illness. Let me share one story with you.

This situation may not appear as a conflict in the conventional way you might think of it, but it is noteworthy. One client wanted to learn knife defense training. We were discussing what I do on the phone, and I asked why knife defense was his primary concern, as that is quite a leap in what I would first teach someone regarding violence prevention. He expressed that he had a violent encounter with his son, who had shown signs of mental illness. After he took his son to the doctor who diagnosed him with bipolar disorder, the doctor gave the son medication. However, the father felt his son might try to harm him. Concerned, he pulled the doctor aside and expressed his fears. The doctor was not concerned once the medication began working. I won't go too in-depth on intuition here, but it is a fundamental topic in all our seminars.

Since the doctor was the "expert," the father felt safer, although the nagging sense of dread of violence from his son continued. Nothing overrules your intuition. That exact evening, the father and son were at the family cottage. The son took a large kitchen knife out of the drawer and told his dad he would kill him. Talk about the most severe of conflicts! The father snatched a club from his golf bag, which was in the doorway by the kitchen. Standing in front of his son, he realized he couldn't hurt him.

See, we don't like to think about it, but confrontation, conflict, and violence may also involve our loved ones. His son was not evil; he has a mental illness. So, the father doesn't want to hurt his son, but he still must protect himself. That evening, the father grabbed a chair and put it between himself and his son. This was such an excellent decision and along the lines of what I would teach. The son was slashing from one side to the other, attempting to cut his father. At one point, he slashed his forearm. The father, during all this chaos, just kept saying out loud without a challenging or threatening tone, "You are killing your father. You are killing your father!" He kept repeating it over and over. At one point, the son stopped, dropped the knife, and rushed out of the cottage. The man called the police, and the son was caught and arrested and is now receiving the proper treatment. The father asked me what he did wrong? "Wrong?" I said. What you said was brilliant; it met all the suggestions we offer in this book.

Even while the son was attempting to kill him, he treated him without the body language, words, or tone that might escalate. Repeating the mantra over and over triggered something in the son's mind to stop. Does that mean I would teach someone in a similar situation to say the same thing? Never—as every scenario has its own challenges, but how this father dealt with his son was optimal considering the circumstances. That is true verbal de-escalation. He got hurt, but he is alive, and the son is now getting treatment and not in jail for murder. That meets the win/win/win goal we want to always seek when possible.

SAFE PROXIMITY

One of the most critical aspects of dealing with anyone you find yourself in conflict with is to keep yourself at a safe distance. If you search "fights" on YouTube, the majority of the time, you'll see two people standing nose to nose, chests puffed out, saying the most immature ego-driven comments or insults in an attempt to intimidate the other person. I will be very frank. This is one of the dumbest and most asinine things you can ever do in any conflict.

It is entirely ego- and emotion-driven with zero strategic value. With someone standing that close to you, you have virtually zero time to react if they do decide to launch an attack, whether it be a punch, shove, headbutt, or assault with a weapon. People think this kind of bravado will intimidate the person into retreat, but that almost never happens. In fact, most times, the escalation is swift and fierce. As my friend Richard Dimitri says, "If you see two people standing toe to toe, you can be assured their fighting IQ is less than zero because you would never let a threat get that close to you!" Besides, it is challenging to carry on and attempt to de-escalate someone standing that close because, again, the body language of conflict does not match the intention of de-escalation if that's what you're genuinely interested in.

One key aspect of managing any conflict is maintaining physical distance because they must move toward you if they do mean you harm, and that offers you a lot of information on their intention. It also provides you time to react, intercept, or move preemptively if the de-escalation is not working. We will offer signs in the next chapter on whether your de-escalation is working.

So, in potential conflict, I suggest you stand well out of arms' reach and keep your hands up in a passive, negotiating stance, as seen here in this picture.

While maintaining distance, if they continue to move forward, never stay stationary. If the person has targeted you, staying in one spot makes you easier to hit. Use the nervous energy you have by moving side to side. Be careful not to move in a straight line going backward. Not only are you more accessible to hit than you would be going side to side, but you might not see any obstacles behind you.

Another advantage of keeping a safe distance from the other person is that you can see both their hands. If you don't see both their hands, you have no idea what they may be concealing. Also, you have less body language to pick up on if they decide to launch an attack.

You want to see all ten fingers in any conflict. In an argument or disagreement, there's no reason someone should appear to be reaching for something behind them. Does their body language match their tone and words? If they're in a productive dialogue with you, quickly reaching behind for something is not common body language.

Other odd observations you might make are one or two hands that remain in their pockets, one arm being held stiff at their side while the other one is up or reaching inside a jacket or clothing. All these are cues to be aware of and why you want to maintain a safe distance if you need to run or defend yourself.

CONFLICT CONTEMPLATIONS

- Do you recall where the conflict took place?
- Was it isolated or public?
- Were there multiple people?
- Did you get close and confrontational or stay at a safe distance?
- Can you think of other variables in the scenario?

CHAPTER 5

THE DO NOTS—PROVOCATION

"Provocation is on the opposite lane of resolution."
—Toba Beta, *Master of Stupidity*

———————————

So, now I hope you understand that it's essential that your body language matches your words and tone; otherwise, you're giving mixed signals whether you're aware of it or not. When it comes to avoiding conflict, here are the Big Do Nots!

Now, I should point out that while I offer these do nots here and dos in the next chapter, it should be noted that anything can work sometimes. Even strategies that I might consider of low value can work in some scenarios. As we've said several times, there are no absolutes in violence prevention, just principles and concepts. If you're using a strategy and it's not working, you need to have the education to switch strategies in an instant. That is easier said than done, but that is the purpose of this book. I will give you the pros and cons of different tactics, and then you can decide what works best for you. As I tell people, you might do something I think would possibly work one out of ten times, but it still worked. It would be irresponsible of me to tell you that you shouldn't have done it if it was successful. But it would also be irresponsible of me to not warn you of what could go wrong if you think that strategy will work every time. I would love to give you one or two strategies that work every time, but there are no assurances. Conflict and confrontation have so many layers to them, so many different types of people, personalities, scenarios, and variables. It's very complex, so we do our best to keep the tactics as basic as possible.

It is essential to point out that conflict can only go one of three ways if it is a one-on-one scenario with no one else involved. Knowing this can lower your chances of freezing up in the moment.

1) You both walk away, agreeing on a solution or agreeing to disagree, but no one gets hurt. This is always the desired outcome.
2) They are going to hit you first.
3) You are going to hit them first.

It is that simple. It can only go one of those ways. So, a circumstantial conflict that could quickly be resolved may turn into a targeted one based on how one or both of you handle it. They may not have intended to target you, but through your dialogue, tone, body language, and emotions, they could decide to take the physical step of harming you if the conflict escalates.

The umbrella term I give to the following do nots is to never say or do anything that will provoke the other person. The dictionary definition of provocation is "to stimulate or give rise to (a reaction or emotion, typically a strong or unwelcome one) in someone."[7] Nothing productive regarding conflict resolution comes from provoking someone. It has the opposite effect, not the desired one if one is looking for a resolution.

Let's look at some of the ways provocation comes into play. Perhaps remember a time you were in a disagreement with someone and felt you had the upper hand right from the start, so you resorted to goading them for no other reason than to see them squirm or get upset. You may have found some joy in it, but at some point, you noticed they were not finding the same humor you were? Provoking someone you know is one thing, but with someone you do not know, it is like playing Russian roulette.

Just like conveying other emotions, you can provoke someone with your body language, tone, and words. And an excellent exercise is to think of times someone has provoked you to get a rise or adverse reaction out of you. How did you feel? In communicating, many will resort to tactics that work on themselves in hopes of getting the same response from the other person. But be very careful what you wish for because their reaction might be less or nonexistent—or it may be too extreme and by the time you notice, too late to reverse. Provocation is a two-way street and a very risky one.

The following all fall under the umbrella term of provocation. Generally, one or both people will deliver a mix of these, not just one. As we go through each, you will notice plenty of overlap. It is essential to explain how they overlap and how stacking two or more contributes to the escalation of a conflict.

---

7   https://www.lexico.com/definition/provoke

- Commanding the other person/telling them what to do
- Asking rhetorical questions
- Making accusations
- Using insults
- Dismissing others' opinions
- Giving physical threat cues
- Issuing challenges or threats
- Telling someone they're wrong
- Getting stuck in the "No, I didn't loop"
- Making the situation about you

COMMANDING THE OTHER PERSON

I am beginning here because it's the most prevalent in conflict. You have a person in front of you, moving toward you, shouting accusations, so you start to feel threatened. You adopt an aggressive stance, your hands up as if preparing to fight, and then you yell, "back off!" or "DO NOT COME ANY CLOSER!"

Now, first, people teach this in self-defense as a strategy to show the person you're dominant and they better not target you or mess with you. But when you command someone with a direct order, you're deeming yourself superior, and often there's an implied threat as well.

We will address threats and challenges specifically, but they are also associated with each subset of provocation. These warnings may be direct or implied.

Conflict resolution commonly teaches that you should be assertive. I'm hesitant to use that term, though. If you look at the dictionary definition of the word assertive, it says, "showing a confident and forceful personality." I have no issue with the word "confident," but the word "forceful" is too strong. In a confrontation, forcing one's personality and opinion on the other person is one-sided and doesn't express the desired result of a win-win-win at heart, in my opinion. I prefer to use the word "confident" as it brings a more appropriate image to the topic. Both may be quite similar, but when I think of the two words and I conjure up an image of both in a confrontation, being confident doesn't project as challenging a picture as being assertive. Remember, we're not talking about a disagreement at work over a business decision but a more heated discussion where accusations are tossed back and forth.

Whether you're assertive or confident, the key is to speak in a respectful, clear, and polite manner.

Being aggressive is the opposite of both assertive and confident. Aggression begets more aggression. When someone facing you is offensive, the goal is to dominate, control, humiliate, and intimidate. This is a quick road to escalation regardless of whether you or the other person is the primary aggressor.

Let's look at the worst-case scenario first—a situation where someone has targeted you for an assault or any form of attack, but it's not an immediate attack but instead through some stage of dialogue. Again, where is this conflict taking place? If it's in public, you decide to use a strategy of a direct command delivered in a loud attention-drawing manner. Yes, you will accomplish attracting attention, and if there is one thing a criminal doesn't want, it's to have attention drawn to the scenario.

In the past, I've taught that the criminal doesn't want attention drawn because they don't want to get caught. In recent years, I've amended that, though. It is true that *typically*, they don't want to get caught, but some don't care if they do and even others simply don't think they will because they're too heavily invested in the conflict with adrenalin and emotion to think clearly enough.

I recall a woman I taught who had been working the bars as a waitress. It was just one of those nights where she had an unusually high number of men making inappropriate, disgusting sexual remarks to her. She had almost become used to it, even accepting it as part of the job. Sober or drunk, many of these men would say things that would make them jump down a person's throat in an instant if they heard them uttered to their own sister, mother, or daughter. Yet, somehow, they seem to find no issue with making these remarks themselves. That is another topic for another book, but anyway, near the end of this woman's shift, she had reached her limit. One guy made a sexual comment, and she swiftly turned to face him. In front of the whole bar, she yelled in exasperation, "Get lost, you creep, and get out of my fucking face!" Wow, talk about going from zero to a hundred in a nanosecond, but if you stack one disgusting remark on top of another, you can imagine how her state of mind and emotions had reached full capacity.

I think we can all understand why someone might explode. Well, it worked. Or did it work? The guy's face immediately turned red as the blood rushed to his face. And in monumental embarrassment, he exited the bar and left. Now, most people would read that and agree that is how you handle conflict. And it can work a certain percentage of the time, but in her case, she, unfortunately, made the same error I made as a young man in my early story; it's an error many people make: she thought the story ended when the guy left.

What she didn't know was when the guy left the bar, his embarrassment turned into rage and anger. I can assure you he was thinking, how dare she treat me like that in front of everyone? She's going to pay for this! So, what did he do?

Many people in his situation would continue home with their tail between their legs, be upset, but not exact any revenge. But not this guy, he decided that her shift must have almost been over since it was later in the evening. So, he waited. He hid where he couldn't be seen and waited for his opportunity to confront her when she left home. He didn't know if she had a car or was walking but figured there was a 50/50 chance she was walking or using public transportation. Well, lucky for him but not for her, she was walking home alone. He followed her and jumped out in front of her rather than ambush her from behind because he wanted her to see his face. He said something to the effect of, "Remember me, bitch? You're not so mouthy now, are you?" and proceeded to sexually assault her off the side of the road before disappearing into the night.

Many will think that while this was terrible, she could easily report it since she knew what he looked like, and he would be arrested. Sadly, it is not that simple if you understand victimization, how few rapists ever go to court, the trauma the victim faces, and the shame they're put through during the whole process. Again, this book is not about that aspect of violence prevention, but it is vital to mention.

I totally appreciate how the woman must have felt, how she reacted, and how he deserved her outburst, but this unfortunate incident illustrates why we need to have multiple strategies available to us. Try to put yourself in her position for a moment. She was not aware that he was a psychopath. The psychopath hates to be humiliated publicly like that. Rather than feeling ashamed, they feel they're dominant and expect to be treated as such. So, when they're not respected, they may take actions accordingly. Their reaction might not always be violent, but it might easily be. And in the case of many psychopaths, they often plan out their revenge, as he did.

So, yes, yelling "back off!" may work, but if you're going to adopt that strategy, be sure to understand the scenario may not be over when you think it is. It may be a couple of hours later, weeks, or even months before you know, but many will want to seek some form of revenge if they've been humiliated or embarrassed, whether privately or in front of a group of people.

What if yelling a command doesn't work? It's hard to reverse from this aggressive approach to the suggestions I will offer. If you start with an extreme like commanding the other person, most of the time you're committed to staying that course. Once again, anything *can* work, but we want to have a toolbox of options most likely to work.

So, why do so many teach to yell "back off!" or some other type of command? That line of thinking is because, on the surface, it appears to make sense and is easy to remember. I mean, Hell yeah, I want them to back off! Simple is good, but it doesn't mean it is the only or best approach.

I like to analyze scenarios from a 360-degree perspective. In other words, you can't just look at it from your perspective, but also must try to understand how the person you are dealing with hears, sees, and interprets your message? Do they believe the implied threat you're making? Does it match your body language? Are you faking it? Faking this so-called badass attitude is a precarious proposition. You might be commanding them, but at the same time have a sheer look of panic in your eyes or on your face. You'll feel fear, but there are cues beyond a reasonable level of anxiety that they might pick up on that will tell them you're faking it. Confidence comes from truly being confident. How do you gain that confidence? Through education like this book; analyzing your past behavior in confrontations; and taking legitimate, realistic, honest training.

Then if you're not faking it when you command the other person, potential witnesses or bystanders might think you're the aggressor. If someone was to come to assist, how would they know who was responsible for the escalation? Remember my brawl? That's not the only time where one or more people have jumped in to help but have aided the troublemaker because they got the wrong signals from what they saw.

Or you may adopt this confrontational strategy, thinking that once you begin commanding and attracting attention (assuming others are nearby), they will rush to your aid. Unfortunately, this is often not what happens.[8] Never rely on anyone else to help or save you. If someone does rush to help, great! But never expect it. As I said, often people will pull out their cellphones and film an incident before they'll physically help you.

If you look at the case of a targeted conflict like rape, which is at the extreme end of violent conflict, most sexual assaults take place somewhere isolated. Remember, if you're targeted, there's a high probability the attacker planned the assault. If they've planned it, they know where and when they will attack, and you

---

8   Remember the famous case of Kitty Genovese where it was reported 38 people heard the screams, but no one helped her? https://www.history. com/topics/crime/kitty-genovese

do not. If you're isolated, adopting the strategy of getting into an aggressive stance and yelling, "back off!" has a higher chance of escalation, as the aggressor sees it as a threat. You're telling them what to do in a situation where they deem themselves superior to you. Telling the "bad guy" what to do is always a risky move.

Also, if your goal in the yelling is to have someone hear you and come running to help, it is unlikely that anyone will hear you if you're isolated. Yelling may also increase the speed with which they attack you, if for no other reason than to shut you up.

So, look at commanding others from a strategic perspective. You adopt a combative stance, and your body language projects that you will harm them if they come any closer. Sure, perhaps you will, but you've also reduced your chance of success because you've taken away any element of surprise you may have had by telegraphing your intention to fight back with both your words and your body language.

This may bring a higher level of violence than they first suspected they needed to gain control of you. Conflict to the extreme like this doesn't begin with your physical tools, but rather your psychological, behavioral, and verbal skills, which can help aid your physical skills if necessary and left with no alternative.

In a targeted attack, if someone does choose you as their victim, they don't see you as a threat. If they decide to target you, it's because they genuinely believe they'll dominate you physically and mentally. Otherwise, they would have chosen someone else. It is critical to understand that attempts to scare or intimidate an attacker once you're selected as a victim often fail miserably.

Yes, commanding can work sometimes, but it's better to use psychology, body language, tones, and words to your advantage.

In a worst-case scenario like this, where you have little to no chance of beating them in a one-on-one fight, your greatest asset is the appearance of vulnerability, making them genuinely believe they've chosen the perfect victim. If they think that you're going to relent and do whatever you want, you may be able to lure them into a high level of overconfidence where they drop their guard, which is the opposite of how they may react if you attempt the badass strategy.

If they think you're complying, the attacker will literally put themself within inches of you without the slightest feeling that you're about to rip them apart. Again, we're not going into any physical concepts in this book, but even in extreme cases of conflict and violence, you still can use verbal strategies to set up your physical defense. In the case of an ambush with no verbal exchange, you're already in the fight and that's not the time to try and talk! But if there is talk previously, you can use certain strategies to increase your chances of survival if you know them, understand them, and know how and when to implement them. I will teach you these strategies.

As I mentioned earlier, commanding or telling another person what to do is still not the smartest strategy, even in a circumstantial conflict where an incident happens unexpectedly. In those cases, you can often literally verbally de-escalate the person if you adopt the proper strategies.

Think of a time someone told you what to do outside of a work environment or personal relationship. Even then, if someone gives you a direct order to do something, you will likely do it, but might think they could have added a please. If we feel just a little bit of annoyance or displeasure in a work environment or relationship, how do we feel or react in a conflict with a stranger who starts telling or commanding us what to do? Not to mention that most often there's an indirect or direct threat with that command. Do this or this will happen.

Here are some examples of commands in conflict. Some are direct and some a bit more subtle, but all can garner the same results of upset, anger, escalation. I have also added what the implied threat might be.

- Back off!—or I will have to do A, B, or C to you.
- Don't come any closer!—or else I will...
- You need to relax!—or there will be consequences.
- Calm down!

We've addressed the harsher commands of "back off!" and "Don't come any closer!" (and similar ones). The two other terms often used in confrontations are some variation of, "You need to relax!" or "Calm down!" Those may sound more like practical verbal de-escalation terms but may result in an even more negative reaction than the brasher commands. Ultimately, you're still telling the other person what to do.

When you've told someone or someone has told you to calm down or relax, has it worked? The person saying it often comes across as being superior. Telling someone to calm down is usually delivered with sarcasm and the implied message that you are in control of yourself, but they are not.

Think about this. Have you ever had a moment of upset with a loved one and at some point, they said, "Look, you need to calm down!" How did that go over? Did you stop, take a deep breath and then calmly keep the discussion going or did you snap back with something like, "I am CALM!" or "Don't tell me to calm down!"

Those expressions may be reactionary and a shield to fear, they may be used intentionally to intimidate, or the person may even say the expression with complete sincerity. But rarely does the phrase ever achieve the desired effect of the person taking a deep breath, taking a step back, and agreeing with you that they need to calm down.

One of the most important lessons to note here is it almost always backfires when we tell our loved ones to calm down. So, to think it would be an effective strategy in a heated argument or disagreement with a stranger who may be accusing you of some wrongdoing is illogical.

People who are uneducated on the topic of verbal de-escalation think words like "calm down," "relax," and "just chill" are de-escalation terms because to relax or calm down is the desired goal. If you tell yourself after a long day at work that it's time to relax, that's an action that is calming and healthy. If you can tell yourself to calm down or relax in a dispute, that's beneficial. But when you begin telling others the same, the message is rarely, if ever, heard the same way.

And to make matters worse, some will add an "or else" to their "Calm down" or "Relax." It may be overtly said or merely implied. Examples might include.

- "Calm down, or I will do it for you!"—more than a little threat there.
- "You better relax before I lose my temper with you!"— You better do this, or you will cause me to do this. They're blaming you if they lose their temper.
- "You need to calm down and shut up or else"—How do most people react? Typically, with an "Or else what?"

I'm not sure they're genuinely fact-gathering but rather meeting the phrase with their own implied threat.

These conversations go round and round with egos clashing and words being thrown around with no one listening. Everyone is fighting to get their next intimidating expression out. Once the dialogue gets to this level, it's tough to regain composure that turns the situation into a productive one.

Another factor is the bystander or third party who might add to the argument you're having with someone else. It could be your friend or theirs, or even a stranger.

If you're in an argument with someone and your spouse overhears, they might say, "Calm down, honey. It's not worth it!" So, this third person is now adding to the dialogue, pulling at you, saying how the situation is not worthy of upset—which may be correct—but the other person might hear that differently. They may hear your ally saying their issue isn't worthy of discussion.

Or even worse, your friend may say, "Calm down. He (or she) isn't worth it!" With your friend or loved one adding the "he" or "she," to the statement, they're saying the other person is not worthy of the discussion or important enough, which could very well feel insulting and disrespectful to someone who is already in a state of upset, anxiety, or anger. That will not help move the conflict toward de-escalation.

To add to all that, you'll often hear people add expressions like "Buddy," "Pal," or the ever popular, "Dude."

"Look, Buddy, you need to calm the eff down!"—So they're calling you their buddy while at the same time telling you to calm down in a manner best described as not calm.

"Look, Brother, you need to chill!"—Ah yes, the term brother. Now, if it is your brother, okay, that might make sense. It isn't usually.

Once again, if either party says this during a heightened conflict, they're telling the other person what to do. Also, most times, people speak like this, using a condescending, "I'm in control" manner with the assumption the other person is not. This might seem like a small thing, but when you add terms like "Buddy," "Pal," or "Brother" in, you may also be adding fuel to the fire. If they're a stranger to you, they may see these terms of endearment as condescending or sarcastic. These are not valuable terms to add to verbal de-escalation attempts.

To highlight the importance of not telling people what to do, use my friend Richard Dimitri's example. You could say, "Just calm down. Have some cake!" and they will probably respond back with, "It's not time for cake!" In other words, it's not so much the words themselves that matter, but the fact is that people don't like to be told what to do, especially not by someone they're arguing with.

Hopefully, you're beginning to see how body language, words, and tone work together to present a complete picture that can work for you or against you. How either party shows themselves is critical in the outcome.

CONFLICT CONTEMPLATIONS

- Can you identify the provocation you have faced in conflict?
- Do you resort to provoking in disagreements?
- What types of provocation listed do you identify with?

ASKING RHETORICAL QUESTIONS

"Do you know who I am? I'm Moe Greene! I made my
bones when you were going out with cheerleaders!"
—The Godfather

In any confrontation, questions about the issue, what happened, what the other party is accusing you of, or vice versa will arise. However, questions, often rhetorical, are not productive during conflict. The following questions have a high likelihood of escalating the emotions of both parties. Read each and picture the body language associated. Have you ever heard or said any of the following questions?

Where did you learn to drive, you idiot?—I'm not sure you're sincerely curious about where they learned to drive, but I could be wrong. In my day, we'd say, "Where did you get your license? In a box of Crackerjack?" I'm confident that it's another insincere one.

Do you know who I am?—This one is still trendy to this day. It tells the other person that the speaker is important, and they're not. It also includes an indirect threat, as if their status will bring forth consequences. A standard reply to that question is something along the lines of, "I don't give a shit who you are!" At that point, both egos are now fully engaged with neither side backing down.

Do you know who my father is?—Similar to the one before, but with a twist. The person is bringing in the importance of their daddy to intimidate or provoke you. Once again, everyone involved knows they're not really asking if you're familiar with the parent and their stature in the community. I recall a video on Instagram with a young punk who was in a bouncer's face outside a nightclub. He was referencing his father as a lawyer and daring the bouncer to engage him physically. His words and body language were challenging and had implied threats behind them.

Well, it worked. The bouncer shoved him to the ground, then multiple people jumped in, and the video ended. This is an interesting example because the bouncer was targeted, but not in the typical way of causing physical harm, but rather to get a reaction to the idea that he might bring financial harm to the victim through the legal system. Again, risky for both people. Whenever physical engagement takes place, the risk of injury is present.

Do you understand what will happen by messing with me?—Still, the question is most often rhetorical but does carry an indirect threat.

Did you not see me when you cut me off in your car?— This is an interesting one because if they did it purposely, they did see you, but if not, it does provide an opportunity to de-escalate if they know what to say. Some will be very tempted to respond sarcastically with something like, "If I had seen you, idiot, I would not have cut you off!" But "I'm really sorry; I didn't see you," might have a better outcome.

What's your problem?—This question is prevalent and most asked in conflict. When asked by a stranger, they're looking for a reason to escalate things if you give them one. Therefore, responses like, "I don't have a problem. What's your problem?" or "I don't have a problem, but you do now!" rarely work to bring any intelligent dialogue forth. Those three words are excellent at triggering someone.

CONFLICT CONTEMPLATIONS

- Have you ever heard or asked these questions in a conflict?
- Were you sarcastic? And if so, what was your intention?
- Do you see how rhetorical questions may escalate conflict?

MAKING ACCUSATIONS

*"When a man points a finger at someone else, he should
remember that three of his fingers are pointing at himself."*
—*Anonymous*

When accusations begin flying, they often swiftly lead to violence. If someone is accusing you of some wrongdoing, their body language, words, and tone will be harsh. The issue at hand may be severe in nature, but many get enraged over seemingly insignificant issues as well, hurling a wide range of possible accusations. These accusations may also come in the form of a question.

Here are a few.

What did you say to me?—Similar to what we discussed with questions, but this one is not likely rhetorical. It has more of an accusatory nature to it. You may or may not have said anything, so it can fall under both circumstantial and targeted conflict. If they genuinely think you said something, your response can take the dialogue in a positive direction or in one that escalates. The person may be looking to start a fight triggered by any excuse. Their justification for hitting you may come if your reply is defensive or flippant. Be very careful to not reply with, "I didn't say anything!" or "I wasn't talking to you!" Both of those do little to begin a productive conversation and, again, picture the body language and tone that is generally behind those words.

Watch where you're going next time!—Maybe you bumped into someone or they bumped into you. Perhaps it was a circumstantial accident or a targeted scenario, with them purposely bumping into you as their entrance to accuse, but either way, this statement implies that they were careless, hardly a de-escalating sentiment.

Were you staring at my girlfriend/boyfriend/significant other?—The accusation is blatant, but whether you did or not is another issue.

Your child just rammed into my car with your grocery cart!—Again, maybe they did or didn't, but either way, you're being accused. When other people are involved in your conflict, particularly children, the emotions can spike instantaneously as one's protective parental nature kicks in.

Watch where you're driving you asshole. You cut me off!—This is a blatant accusation, again, whether you did cut them off or not. We'll discuss this in more depth when talking about road rage.

CONFLICT CONTEMPLATIONS

- Have you ever accused someone of something? How did they respond?
- How do you respond to accusations you are guilty of or not?

USING INSULTS

"A wise man is superior to any insults which can be put upon him, and the best reply to unseemly behavior is patience and moderation."
—Moliere

One of the quickest ways to find someone's fist connecting with your jaw is to insult or belittle them. When you get personal, you've taken the focus away from the issue at hand and turned it into a grade one child argument. Name-calling should never occur in a confrontation between two supposed adults. People resort to insults when they lose control and are making a last-ditch attempt to control the other person. Do I need to point out some examples? Okay, how about:

- You stupid idiot.
- Hey, moron, you don't have a clue what you're talking about.
- What's your IQ there, Einstein?

Can you think of a time when someone insulted you and you lost your mind? Of course, you can. So why do you think anyone else will accept your insults?

VERBAL "FIGHT OR FLIGHT"

When one senses they're "losing" a conflict, they often resort to a verbal fight or flight. The person may become defensive or fight back with insults, as mentioned. When I say "flight" in conflict, running away might be an excellent response if the option is available.

DISMISSING OTHERS' OPINIONS

When you dismiss what someone is saying to you before getting all the facts, you're disrespecting the other person, and it's another form of insulting them. It shows you're not listening. Therefore, I suggest to keep quiet and not say the first words that come to their lips. Listen and then reply, but do not dismiss. Not only is dismissing others' opinions inherently antagonistic but most dismissive comments are made with sarcasm. Sarcasm has no place in confrontation. Some will blow it off and say they're just joking, but that also tells the person you're not taking their issue seriously. Dismissing also comes with body language that matches the disrespect. The ego loves to deny what others have to say.

Examples of dismissive comments may include:
- What the hell do you know anyway?
- Do you have any clue what you're talking about?
- Could someone please tell me what they're trying to say?

GIVING PHYSICAL THREAT CUES

Finger-Pointing—A typical action when someone is accusing someone else is the art of finger-pointing. Take any of the previous statements, and you can picture the aggressor pointing directly at the person they're accusing. In addition to the words and tone of those statements, having a finger directed at you or right in your face adds to making the threat personal. Finger-pointing is used to intimidate and take away your ability to deflect any responsibility. How do you feel when someone points at you? Does it help to calm you down or just the opposite? Exactly. So, I suggest you lose finger-pointing if it's part of your verbal de-escalation toolbox.

Clenching Fists—Another common physical reaction, offering several cues to escalation, is making a fist. If you approach with your fists clenched, you are offering them a physical cue you might want to fight, not de-escalate. So, opening and closing your fists during the dialogue, shows you are building up, not calming down. Clenching of fists is a threat both parties might pick up on. Take that body language cue very seriously as it's a significant sign.

Looking Around—If either of you clench your fists, begin finger-pointing, then looking away in a different direction, there's a high probability one is searching for witnesses before becoming physical. Many will check the environment first before striking. If someone is looking for resolution, they should be looking at you, engaged in the conversation. So, don't look around in a confrontation; otherwise, your opponent may worry you are about to strike.

Looking away or just off to the side of you is an excellent distraction technique. You can even try this. Next time you're speaking with someone in a normal conversation, take your glance off to one side, just a bit. Virtually every single time, that person will wonder what you're looking at, and then turn their head to see. This strategy can be used for good or evil. Evil if the person does it to distract you before hitting you. And useful if you use it for the same strategy if you have no other options left to avoid violence.

Cellphones—Cellphones are an excellent safety device if you need to report a crime, call 911 or get a picture that may help the police. But they can also be used to threaten someone, as I will reference in more detail in the next section about challenges and threats. Do not pull out your cellphone and begin recording thinking they will instantly end the conflict. In conflict, they will see your recording of them as a direct threat.

Most often, when the person directly involved in the conflict is pointing their cellphone, they are saying something like, "Keep coming at me, buddy. I have it all on video for the police!" Of course, different things might be said; the actual words might be different, but the phrases all have the same meaning or sentiment. You are telling the person they are wrong, and you have the evidence to prove it. There are multiple threats and challenges involved by pulling out your phone and recording a conflict.

I'm not saying having evidence of some wrongdoing is necessarily bad but understand how and when you do it matters and assess how the aggressor interprets it. Look at it from the perspective of the other person. If they're wrong, they see your cellphone and know you have evidence of their actions. So now most likely, they want that phone and will probably do anything to get it out of your hands. And most of the time, the tone of the words being used by the person recording is sarcastic and condescending because they are confident once they video, the person will stop advancing. It's incredible how many people think that recording someone already in a heightened state of anger and aggression, possibly fueled by drugs or alcohol, is going to reach a logical conclusion that their actions are wrong.

ISSUING CHALLENGES & THREATS

How dare you speak to us like that! —ego

I have clearly shown most conflicts have challenges and threats built into them through body language or words and the tone of those words. You can see how the threats are said directly or may be implied. Most of these challenges are along the lines of telling someone to do something "or else"—or else there will be some sort of unpleasant consequence.

The benefit of someone giving you a direct challenge with an or else is that it leaves little to wonder what their intentions are. Hearing this helps you immensely when determining your strategy. And if witnesses can hear the words being exchanged, that can also be of great benefit, whether they decide to help you, or explain to a police officer or judge what they heard. Otherwise, it's your word against the other person's.

It is essential to remind you again that challenges and threats may be coming from both people, not just the aggressor. Examples may include.

If you come any closer, I'll call the police!—This one may intimidate your aggressor into stopping, but what if it doesn't, and, in fact, enrages them further? To think the person charging toward you is going to stop and think, "Hmmm, I better stop as I do not want to be arrested" can be a risky proposition. By offering this ultimatum, you're also saying they're in the wrong, which might not be appreciated. You're playing commander-in-chief by using an expression like this, deeming yourself as the one in charge, and it can be a risky strategy.

You don't have the balls to say that to my face!—I can't say I've heard many women say this one, but men say it often. Or they may simply say, ***Come say that to my face!*** Whether you say it, or the other person does, what is the implication? It's very challenging with an underlying message that you're a coward, not a "man," scared, afraid of me, and so on. It hits a nerve for many people and can bring on instant escalation in the conflict. Many will hear a challenge like that and snap with a physical response, which is precisely what the other person may be looking for. Think of it as a puppet show. If someone can control you with their body language, words, and tone, then you have little chance to de-escalate. But if you can identify with phrases like this, understand them, and really want to avoid any escalation, you have a chance to bring peace to the conflict. As said earlier, statements like these are only words, and they only have the power over you that you let them.

An extreme version of the above phrase, which admittedly is rarer but does happen occasionally if one person pulls out a knife or some other weapon is,

You don't have the balls to use that!—Unfortunately, too often seconds later, the person who yelled that challenging phrase finds themselves with a new hole in their body, not having believed for a second the other person would call them on that challenge. Even the person guilty of doing the stabbing may be in shock. But when the ego is challenged, many will rise to that challenge.

Again, recall when I said we would make a different decision if we could see into the future? This example falls precisely in that category. Decent people who have taken action similar to this, for a split second, were caught in the high intensity of a moment, felt challenged, dared, and disrespected only to find themselves taking the most extreme of actions and destroying lives in an instant. Often, they can't even believe they did it. Once we lose control of our emotions, we cannot think or act rationally. Add a weapon to this, and you have a dangerous cocktail.

So, would people say something so stupid? Because in a million years, they never expected the person to use the weapon. If they had, they wouldn't have said it. But as previously mentioned, if you don't know the person in front of you, their history, their experiences, their present or ongoing mental state, you can't know whether they'll back down. Because your threats work 95 percent of the time, that is no guarantee they will work 100 percent of the time. And the one time it doesn't, death is a possibility, whether intended or not.

CONFLICT CONTEMPLATIONS

- What is challenging and threatening to you?
- How might you react to these threats and challenges?
- Are they more likely to escalate or de-escalate a conflict?

TELLING SOMEONE THEY'RE WRONG

You may be right, but don't tell them they are wrong.

Telling someone they're wrong is rarely, if ever, effective in handling any confrontation or conflict. Even if you know with absolute certainty the other person is wrong, expecting them to instantly agree and discontinue the disagreement is unrealistic. Even crazier is that some realize they're in the wrong but will fight until the end anyway, to save face.

If one was to point out in a calm, productive back and forth conversation with examples, thoughtfulness, and a desire to really hear the other person's message, you might come around to see where you might be wrong. But not many confrontations play out quite like that. Just hearing the word "wrong" is a trigger for many. It often throws up a wall that will be tough to tear down. Avoid all these ways of telling people they're wrong:

You're wrong!—Direct and to the point. Imagine the body language, facial expressions, and tone people might say this with.

That's all wrong!—Just in case the person had any doubt, this one tells the other person everything about the situation is wrong. While not as direct without the word "you," adding the "all" makes up for it.

No, you've got it wrong!—A direct attempt to stop you. This statement gets personal with the "you," followed by the position that you're not right. You can see how one word here or there can make it more personal or direct and bring more passion, emotion, and potential for escalation of the issue.

That's stupid. You're wrong!—This one has the added implication that the other person is being stupid. This is a surefire way not to calm them down or initiate some intelligent dialogue.

I could go on and on with these phrases, but I hope you see the pattern in them and how they rarely work if the goal is verbal de-escalation.

GETTING STUCK IN THE "NO, I DIDN'T" LOOP

*Saying no is a complete sentence but expecting
the other person to honor that is risky.*

This is a trap most of us have fallen into. It may rarely result in physical harm in a conversation with someone we respect or love, but in conflict with someone accusing you of something you didn't do, just saying you didn't do it repeatedly is unproductive.

Let's take a simple example. Imagine someone accusing you of staring at their partner. You were looking over in that direction, but you weren't staring at them.

They come over, get in your face, and say something like, ***"Why are you staring at my wife?"*** Many immediately get their back up when questioned like this. They get defensive and often are rude in their body language, expressions, and reply, especially if they weren't doing what they were accused of. If the response is loud and attention is drawn, you now have the added factor of an audience, which may or may not be beneficial to de-escalation. I say beneficial in that with added people, they may attempt to break up the conflict. On the other hand, people may take sides, or one person might have more backup than the other. Again, multiple unpredictable variables can affect the scene.

You reply, ***"I wasn't staring at your wife. What are you talking about?"***—This is a very common reply, but one that instantly challenges the accuser. Think about it. They're already angry and jealous, and you tell them they're wrong, then question their question to begin with. Imagine your body language, tone, and words if this were you.

They may reply something along the lines that they saw you staring at her and ask you if you're calling them a liar. So, do you see the slow or quick escalation that may occur? They accused you of something, you told them you didn't do it with less than optimal communication skills, and then they up the ante by claiming you challenged their integrity.

You may insist over and over that you didn't do what they accused you of but repeating the same answer in different ways won't change their mind. It's futile and adds fuel to the fire. This is an example of a frequent confrontation that moves to conflict and often violence. And it is stupid, silly, immature, and can be wholly avoided assuming the accuser is not using it as an excuse to use force. If it is genuinely a circumstantial scenario, it can be quickly defused if your ego is in check and you remember that any conflict can end horribly.

The next chapter will give you proactive steps to take when these issues all come up. But for now, the primary message is that if you say anything—through your words, tone, or body language—that might provoke the other person, you're setting yourself up for failure.

CONFLICT CONTEMPLATIONS

- How do you feel when someone tells you that you are wrong?
- How do people react when you tell them they are wrong?
- The goal should be to get home safely, not prove the other person wrong!

MAKING THE SITUATION ABOUT YOU

Saying "I" defensively is the first brick in a conflict wall.

When we defend ourselves and our actions, immediately resorting to "I" in a defensive manner is the first step in creating a wall, not tearing one down. As you'll see in the next chapter, seeking knowledge of the issue from the other person's side is more productive. The words "I" and "you" are concise, but powerful words that need to be used strategically. Have you ever said any of these lines?

I did not cut you off!—Using the word "I" makes it more personal and threatening to the other person. Using "I" emphasizes that you would never, or are not capable of, what they're accusing you of.

I'm going to give you three seconds to get out of my face!—You've given a direct command with boundaries, consequences, and superiority by using the word "I."

I don't care what you think!—Again, this puts the emphasis on yourself as superior to the other person and then diminishes them by not caring what they think.

It's difficult to not refer to yourself when accused of something, but as you will see in the next chapter, the more you can make the discussion about them, the more productive the dialogue will be.

CHAPTER 6

ALL THOSE DO NOTS.
WHAT SHOULD I SAY OR DO?

*This moment of conflict in front of you
is much more than the present.*

It has implications for your future!

I have thrown several do nots at you. So, what *should* you do and say? Some examples of ways to react that are not likely to escalate a conflict are:

- Always be nice
- Always ask, "How Can I Help You?"
- Always listen
- Always show empathy
- Always be accountable
- Always aim for Win/Win/Win
- Always remember the costs

Some of these will challenge your ego, but they're fundamental if you wish to reach the objective in conflict resolution.

ALWAYS BE NICE

Remaining nice in the face of conflict is extremely challenging for most people. You're face to face with someone; they're blaming you for something they think you did. They're angry, frustrated, anxious, and losing control of their emotions.

Your ego may order you to stand up and not take this abuse.

To quote Patrick Swayze's character from the movie, *Roadhouse,* "I want you to be nice until it's time to not be nice." It might seem like a trivial statement, but it adds so much value to this topic.

I'm not suggesting you be happy and jovial in a moment of conflict. But, the power of being friendly will put you further ahead of most people.

Think of the alternative. By not being nice, what chance is there of de-escalating the scenario? Intimidating or scaring someone into backing down may seem like a successful strategy. But it can be risky and does not meet the desired goal of win/win/win.

That is verbal intimidation, not verbal de-escalation. Yes, anything can work occasionally, but very few can pull off that level of intimidation. And if it does not work, you will have a hard time taking a few steps back and switching your approach. Once you resort to intimidation, you're committed. It may work for you most of the time, but then one day you just might meet that one person who isn't intimidated.

Yes, many professional bouncers are skilled in applying intimidation. That is a unique work environment, to be sure. But there is still a benefit in being friendly with the clients until otherwise. You are not a professional bouncer, so it is better to be kind.

Being kind, not sarcastic, can set the tone from the outset. They might snap out of their anger when you don't jump to a defensive, aggressive, defiant position.

You might see their body language change or the pace and tone of their words. If they have an issue with you and you're friendly, there's no reason for them to lose their cool unless you give them a reason to.

Do not mistake being helpful as being submissive or weak, either. Being helpful and remaining calm can be a non-challenging display of confidence.

With your palms up, open-handed, showing them, you prefer to resolve the issue, there's no reason for them to feel a threat.

PIC OF PASSIVE STANCE

This picture shows someone who looks nonthreatening. It is hard to look at this picture and think this man wishes to start a fight, argue, or escalate matters. Now, your body language is just as important as the words you use; they need to match.

If you give mixed signals, the person will see the body language and determine their next step or terms from that.

Accepting being friendly and kind is the initial step in success. It doesn't mean they're right and you're wrong. But what if you *were* wrong?

CONFLICT CONTEMPLATIONS

- Does the adage "Treat others the way you would like to be treated" ring true in your life?
- If not, look at yourself and ask yourself, Why?
- Consider a time you were friendly to someone in conflict. Did it escalate the scenario, help, or at least level off?

THE POWER OF "I AM SORRY!"

Never ruin an apology with an excuse.
—unknown

If someone accuses you of something *you did do*, how about apologizing? Wow, what a concept to say, "I am sorry!" Those three single words can stop most disputes or conflicts in their tracks. By admitting guilt, you're not giving in; it's the contrary. You're showing maturity and accountability. Here are examples of different types of apologies that could occur.

— *"You cut me off, I almost went in the ditch, you stupid moron!"*

"I'm sorry, you're right. I didn't see you. I hope you're okay. Again, I'm sorry!"

— **"Watch where you're going! You almost knocked me into traffic!"**

"I was in a hurry and didn't see you. I'm sorry!"

— **"Your dog keeps running off its leash, and my kids are playing. What if it attacks my children?"**

"Oh my God! I am sorry. I understand why you're angry. I'll get a stronger leash."

— *"Stop staring at my girlfriend before I knock you into tomorrow!"*

"Sorry I was drifting off into space and didn't realize I was staring at her. I'm happy to apologize to her if I made her uncomfortable."

We could go on and on with scenarios where you have someone in front of you, heated, upset, and accusatory.

If you apologize, many times, the crisis doesn't escalate any further. The other party may not be all smiles and walk away with no problem, but the goal is to part ways with no one getting hurt. Sounds simple, right?

Then why is it such a struggle for so many, even when they're wrong and they know it, to say they're sorry?

Many will give an excuse in the face of proof they were wrong. Many feel apologizing is a threat to their sense of self. They may feel shame. People don't want to look stupid or weak. They get defensive and come up with the body language, words, and tone that are the opposite of being sorry.

Someone who lacks confidence in themselves might struggle to say they're sorry, whereas the confident person has no issue offering an apology. Saying you're sorry shows character. It shows you are secure and accountable for your actions.

Many offer an apology out of guilt. But some people don't want to appear inferior, and they fear that saying they're sorry displays that. For others, apologizing doesn't fit their psychological makeup. They would rather fight tooth and nail to avoid having to take a serious look at themselves.

Another reason it is tough to accept guilt is the worry of escalation. You may fear that the other person may look at your wrongdoing as a reason to punish you. So, some think it's better to stand their ground.

Others will say they're sorry, but not mean it. How you deliver, "I am sorry" will appear through your body language.

Despite all the excuses, it is the proper thing to do and understanding this produces a high chance of resolving the conflict.

If you did not do what they are accusing you of, saying you're wrong may still be a good strategy. Offer an apology if you determine that you could get hurt based on the variables of the scenario.

In a higher-risk environment like a bar, it may be smart for no other reason than self-preservation. Particularly if you're outnumbered.

Apologizing is healthy for both parties. It reduces the chances of a tragic result for all concerned.

In targeted conflict, however, saying you're sorry will not work. The instigator is looking to pick a fight. But if you do apologize and it goes unaccepted, that information still gives you a lot of insight as to what and whom you are dealing with.

What if you have a car accident? You get out of your vehicle and see four large muscular individuals. Saying sorry may not be sincere, but it might be strategic. You must appear sincere, though, which will be reflected through your body language, followed by the words, and then tone.

Saying you're sorry with sarcasm is worse than not even saying you are sorry to begin with.

You probably understand saying sorry if you've done something improper, but you will not say it if you're innocent. People will stand on principle despite the obvious risks presented to them.

If the crisis involves any chance of a financial cost, many will not apologize. But if your instinct or the precontact cues show a high chance of harm, it's better to swallow your pride, say you're sorry, and escape the immediate risks.

Let's take another example since so many people are very passionate about their cars.

You're in a grocery store. You've parked your vehicle, and you get out of your driver's side door. Beside you is a beautiful brand-new Dodge Challenger 2020. Owning one has been a dream of yours, which is why you parked so close to it that you could get an up-close view. Once out of the car, you notice there is a 2-foot scratch on its passenger door. Immediately you feel sorry and empathize with the person who must own the vehicle. Damn, I would be upset if that was me. Poor guy or gal who owns the car.

Well, approaching the vehicle is the owner of the car. You tell them you love the car and say something like, "Shit, sorry to see someone has already scratched it, you must be angry!"

They scream, *"What? A scratch? Where?"* They run to the passenger side. In a state of rage, they assume you must have done it as it appears the scratch is the same color as your car. They scream, ***"How did this happen, why the hell did you get so close to my car? I just bought it!"***

But you did not scratch it and you get defensive. "I didn't scratch it, I assumed you knew. I had nothing to do with it. I just parked close to get a closer look, but I haven't touched it!"

They get angrier, closing the distance between you and them. You yell, ***"Back off, buddy. I told you I had nothing to do with it!"***

See how the encounter could escalate? It could even lead to a physical fight. The person accusing you is in a heightened state of anxiety—and your remarks are adding fuel to the fire.

But while you read this, can you understand their assumption you must have done it? Is it conceivable you might have acted the same way if you were to switch positions? Here is where feeling some empathy might help, as it might guide your words further.

This is an instance where you say you're sorry, not to accept blame or responsibility but to take away some anger directed straight at you. It may not work, but it's worth a try rather than the opposite. You might say something like,

"I don't know how it happened, but I understand you're upset and can see why you think it was me. I would feel the same too. This sucks. I am sorry this happened."

All the while, as you say this, heed my earlier advice on maintaining a safe distance. Keep your hands up in a passive, negotiating stance, not a fighting stance. Your stance must be congruent with the scenario. It's important to show an empathetic look of understanding on your face.

Keep your hands up in case they're close. The other party may lose control. They might grab, shove, or strike you out of certainty you damaged their car.

If you can, position yourself with a barrier. Keep your hood or the whole car between you. You'll be at a much safer distance barring them having a weapon like a gun. With the distance, they may see the scratch and conclude it could not have been you. Or they might begin a dialogue searching for evidence that it couldn't have been you. Regardless, their first words will provide direction on which way this may go.

This may be a circumstantial conflict, but it could become a targeted one based on your response. If they conclude it had to be you, they might feel you need to pay for this. In a case like this, you may even offer a solution that meets their assumption that it was you. You could say something like, ***"I understand why you think I did it, so let's call the police so we can get this sorted out."***

You might not use those exact words but making the offer to get the police involved doesn't tell them they are wrong. It also tells them you understand why they're upset.

You know that you did not do it and hopefully proving it will not be difficult. This is not the moment while they're in their irregular state of mind.

Now, a few things might take place. Their intensity level might sink. They might gain some of their logical thinking back. They may be annoyed and angry still, but not directed at you anymore. Now, they may ask, how did this happen? Who the hell did it?

But they also might keep reiterating it was you. They could get further upset because in their mind it *had* to be you. It is futile after a couple of friendly attempts to reach their logical brain once they have made up their mind. But still, you must resist the temptation to become defensive.

You might start to think you were helpful and wonder why they're still yelling at you. You may even conclude, to hell with it and unleash on them. Resist the urge. Waiting for the police to show up is your best hope for a successful result.

Maybe you can go into the store to wait? Make sure you find a location that isn't isolated where you can wait for the police.

The variables of each scenario will always dictate your best response. If you can't exit, then there is a high likelihood that the conflict will become physical. Do your best to de-escalate or remove yourself.

A NOTE ABOUT VERBAL DE-ESCALATION

Verbal de-escalation is your best defense against a conflict getting out of control. As I have mentioned before, there are no guarantees, though, when it comes to conflict. Verbal de-escalation can be like navigating a minefield. You never know which word, body movement, or use of your tone might ignite rage from the other person. It comes back to what I said earlier about not knowing the person in front of you. As mentioned, several times, there are no guarantees.

The word "sorry" could even trigger them. What if, as a child, their father or mother never viewed their apologies as sincere? They may have been on the receiving end of more abuse for saying they were sorry. So now, when they hear the word, it has no meaning and, in fact, triggers them to deliver consequences.

I can't emphasize this enough: unless you know the person, you have no way of knowing what their triggers are.

CONFLICT CONTEMPLATIONS

- Think of a time you apologized. How did the other person react?
- Think of a time someone apologized to you. How did you feel?
- Never underrate the strength of apologizing in conflict.

FACT-FINDING WITH THE QUESTION, "HOW CAN I HELP YOU?"

Don't say what you're thinking!
Listen first to understand, then speak!

A compelling question you can use in any confrontation or conflict is, "How can I help you?" It meets all the criteria of effective verbal de-escalation. You ask what the issue is without challenging, threatening, or commanding them. And saying, "you" shows you understand *they* have a problem and *you* want to know what it is so *we* can resolve it. In a circumstantial confrontation, if you ask that question, what you should see and hear is the other person stopping, then stating what the exact issue is. The next step is listening with an honest desire to hear what the problem is. We know it might make perfect sense when you read it here, but in the moment it's often easier said than done.

I believe there is much more value in sharing the stories where we mess up and make mistakes. The goal is to learn from our own stories and those shared with us. As Richard Dimitri always points out, we are all human and at the mercy of our emotions. One might be a prolific leading authority on violence prevention, but if they are having a shitty day, that will come into play if they find themselves in a confrontation. Even the experts are human and at the mercy of their emotions like anyone else. We all do our best to manage them or snap out of them, but no one is perfect. And sometimes, the person you conflict with, even if they have zero experience in verbal de-escalation, might be the one to snap you out of it. I have mentioned Richard Dimitri several times. This story illustrates this very well.

Many years ago, before he became enlightened to the importance of psychology, he was at a bar blowing off some steam with his friends. He went to order a few shots of liquor, and the bartender filled each shot glass up to the rim. So full, they were dripping down the sides a bit. Richard took all three shot glasses with his two hands. When he moved to turn around, another gentleman bumped into him by accident, overflowing the drinks down the sides of his hands. Richard's immediate reply because he was suffering a less than an optimal day was, "Watch where the fuck you are going!" The man apologized, stating, "I am so sorry; let me get you some new drinks." Though not happy, Richard said, "No, that is fine, don't worry about it." The guy insisted again that he would replace the drinks, but Rich declined and walked away, telling the man not to worry about it.

The man snapped Richard out of his initial anger and made him realize it was just a mistake and not worthy of knocking the guy out. This was a circumstantial confrontation. I am sure the other guy did not leave his home that night and plan to bump into someone, spill their drinks, and then make them feel small for reacting out of proportion to what took place. But if that guy had studied in a combative type system, the moment Richard said, "Watch where the fuck you are going!" it could have played out differently.

If Richard had learned to not accept crap from anybody, he might have launched into an assault. The familiar saying "Hit first, ask questions later" is a common, but very risk attitude. Also, what if you punch the guy, knock him out, and his head smacks the bar? And you have fifty witnesses to what resulted? You expect any court will agree with your explanation for flattening the guy out and leading to severe injury was lawful because the other guy cursed at you after you bumped into him?

Similar stories play out every day all over the world with disastrous results. Often by respectable people who are just having a lousy day, never imagining the result for them, the person they conflicted with and their extended families and friends.

Instead of finding yourself in that situation, asking "How can I help you"? will take you in a better direction: either toward settling it or helping you recognize it will not matter what you say; they have determined in their mind to target you for whatever their intentions are.

The back and forth might go on for several minutes or give you the answers you need. For example, if you ask.

How Can I Help You?—They reply something like, ***"Nothing, you piece of shit!"*** while moving toward you with violent body language and precontact clues, talking over you, not letting you get a word in edgewise. Well, you have your answer.

If they have told you there is nothing you can say or do and are about to hit you, do not force any more verbal de-escalation. Verbal de-escalation is like navigating a field of landmines; you can't always impose a precise direction.

REALLY LISTEN

Foremost, listen to understand the other person, not to plan your defense to what they are saying. If you are coming up with your argument before hearing them, you are not listening with the goal of resolution.

Let's say you think they are mistaken with their accusation, but you have resisted stopping them mid-sentence or saying they are wrong. One way to begin the analysis of their blame is to wait until you have listened to them, and then say, "Okay, let me make sure I understand what you are saying."

We call this paraphrasing, and by saying that, you're telling them you were listening and now you want to get crystal clear on what they said. If they let you talk, that is an excellent sign and provides you some control of the communication. It also shows that they may want to resolve the issue. If they still do not let you talk, or they talk over you or escalate the threat with their body language, words, and tone, that gives you a lot of information that they may target you.

Also, if there are observers, they can attest that you showed empathy and told them you wish to understand what they said. Careful with what you say, though, as your words can either harm you or support you when recounted to the police if they become involved.

It may take some time, but with an eagerness to learn, when you speak or listen, you will notice cues in others' body language that will be valuable. If you speak and their body appears to relax and drop in intensity and their outward expressions changes, showing less irritation or anger, these good signs show you're on the right path. They may no longer be clenching their teeth or flailing so much. They might even apologize that they flew off the handle once they see your reactions and replies.

Where their anger was initially directed at you, it may now come out that they were more upset or disappointed because of the day they were having. Perhaps something in their lives was weighing on their minds and it built to a point where they just lost it. So, it was not you but rather the culmination of circumstances in their life. But without you being a listening, empathetic partner in this dispute, it may end up in a life-altering decision that one or both may regret later. We are at the mercy of our emotions often.

CHAPTER 7

HOW TO ANSWER QUESTIONS

"Statements often bring controversy.
Questions often bring unity."
— Emilyann Allen

Those questions they ask you might be sarcastic, rhetorical, or used to get under your skin. However, you can use their questions to your advantage. The most frequent questions I see and hear in conflict are.

- **What's Your Fuckin' Problem?** The temptation and common reply to this question is something like, "I don't have a problem. What's your problem?" This will not de-escalate anyone. It is often used to elicit a response from you to justify the next actions they're planning to take. If you want to de-escalate, you might respond with something like, "I have a lot of problems. Does it show on my face?" Now, they may react with something like, "Are you kidding me?" if they think you are sarcastic. But perhaps you will create a small opening to begin some dialogue. If the person is, as my friend Richard Dimitri says, a reasonable person having a bad day, they may pause for a moment allowing you to state your problem. Or they might not care, but their reply will give you a lot of information. There are many de-escalating responses, but here are a few:

- Sorry, I was having a crap day at work, and I got fired, so I can understand why you feel I was looking at you with some anger. It is not you; it's the day I'm having. Sorry, I have no problem with you at all.

- Yeah, I just found out A, B, or C, and I was here blowing off some steam. Maybe we got our messages crossed. I am sorry if I looked at you like I had an issue with you. My fault.

- I've got more problems than you want to hear about, but not with you. Sorry!

See, if you answer their question, but in a fashion that doesn't challenge them, you're presenting an opportunity for them to save face, and maybe—just maybe —you will reach their empathetic side. They may even laugh and show you they understand. Hell, they may also ask more questions to show you they're sorry for jumping to conclusions.

As I have said many times, when posed a question like "What's your problem?" resist the urge to say what comes to your mind. Listen to the question, take the sarcasm out of it, and then reply.

A story from Richard Dimitri illustrates this. Years ago, he was at a bar in Montreal waiting for a friend to arrive. While he was waiting, he noticed two gentlemen playing pool in another section of the bar. They appeared to be more than proficient, so to kill some time until his friend came, Richard watched from a distance. While the one guy bent over to take his next shot, the other man huddled next to him and whispered something to his friend, but they were too far away for Richard to hear what was being said.

They stood up and glanced over at Richard with a blank stare. Richard knew from experience that this was not a good sign. (Note, in hindsight this would have been the perfect time to leave the bar, but he didn't.) The one guy walked toward Richard with the pool cue in his grasp, by his side. As he got close, he stopped and said to Richard, "What's your fuckin' problem." Many people might get their back up with some smart-ass remark. Instead, Richard said, "I have a lot of problems. Why, does it show on my face?"

Uncertain, the guy came back with, "Are you fuckin' kidding me?" He was asking in his own eloquent way if Richard was being sarcastic. Richard replied, "No, just last week, I left work early to surprise my fiancé because I spend a lot of time travelling for work. When I opened the door thinking I would be a pleasant surprise, I found her right there in my living room having sex with some guy!"

The guy asked Richard, "Did you kill the guy?" Richard replied, "No, it's not the guy's fault and better to find out now before getting married." The guy said, "Shit, man, I'm sorry to hear that." Richard explained he came to the bar to blow off some steam.

Richard already noticed a substantial shift in the guy's body language. When he first came over, he was walking tall in an aggressive strut with his chest puffed out. But by that point, he was a few feet from Richard with his hands down, his body more relaxed, and conveying empathy with his words and tone. So, it was clear Richard had already taken significant steps toward avoiding any further conflict. But the guy's buddy was looking over from a distance wondering why nobody was fighting. So over he came with a similar strut and forceful nature. Richard again prepared himself in case this guy wasn't as empathetic. Before he got too close, the friend stopped him and relayed Richard's story to him. Again, the question came, "Did you kill the guy?" After a few more words, both guys held a normal friendly conversation with Rich. When Rich's friend arrived, they played a couple of games of pool. It turned out they were there for similar reasons.

Now I ask you, would you have had a similar reaction to Richard or quite different? Because of his confidence and prior experience with violence, he could handle this in a way to avoid a fight at all costs, knowing how a situation like this can go wrong for him and these guys. Now, could it still have become a fight? For sure, but why jump to that stage without attempting to de-escalate it first?

This story is like countless scenarios that play out every day, but those often have tragic results.

It also reminds me of a time I was teaching one of my women's self-defense parties. I had a group of about six women, and we were discussing conflict resolution. One woman was asking some fantastic questions. At one point, she said, "Chris, this all makes perfect sense. But if the other person is wrong, do you not think I could point out their mistake so they will understand the life lesson I taught them when they get home and reflect?" I chuckled and said, "No, it is not your job to teach someone any lesson. Your job is to get home to your family!"

When you attempt to teach someone a lesson, even with the best of intentions, most often, you will come across as thinking you're superior to them. Acting superior is not a useful tool in resolving any disagreement and will make matters worse.

It is very essential to understand that you are not there to teach lessons or to prove someone wrong. I repeat: your only goal is to get home with no harm to anyone involved. If they reflect on the matter later in the day and learn a valuable lesson, great! But that's not your goal.

OVERCOMING OBJECTIONS

"An objection is not a rejection;
it is simply a request for more information."
—Jo Bennett

In any conflict, people will have objections. If accepting responsibility and saying you're sorry is enough, great, but don't expect it. In fact, try to have no expectations during confrontation, conflict, and violence. I say this because, if you expect a specific result and it does not come to fruition, you're more prone to freeze. But if you understand that conflicts can go in many directions, you can navigate word to word as you listen and respond. If one is giving you objections but is speaking at a safe distance, that is an excellent sign that you are on the right track.

When you hear the objection, but a question is attached to it, then the objection wasn't fully rejected. Or you might hear some doubt in their objection, presenting an opening for resolution. Examples might be.

- I found this parking spot before you. What makes you think you were here first?
- My wife said you were staring at her. I didn't see you, but she said you did. Were you?
- Your dog just took a crap on my lawn and you did not pick it up. I assume it was your dog!

CAREFUL WITH YOUR *BUT*

I've pointed out a few times that seldom should we say the initial thought that comes to our minds. In overcoming objections, people often say "but," accompanied by their opposition, even before the other person has completed their complaint or accusation. When you say "but" to someone, you're dismissing what they just said.

Thus, it comes across as another type of challenge. And if you say it before they've finished what they were saying, you've included impoliteness to your objection—as if you weren't listening to anything they said, and then adding that you don't agree. It is a classic defense mechanism many people use, but a trigger for the person you're saying it to.

As I've noted, if your goal is to resolve the issue at hand, you must *listen* before replying. Throwing "buts" in before the other person finishes or cutting them off mid-sentence with a "Let me stop you right there!" is almost sure to upset them. People want to be understood. So, you need to understand them first rather than attempt to force them to understand you. Do not make the confrontation about you. Understand, first. Then state your case.

CHAPTER 8

ROAD RAGE

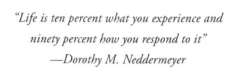

> *"Life is ten percent what you experience and*
> *ninety percent how you respond to it"*
> —*Dorothy M. Neddermeyer*

I wanted to designate a chapter to road rage. Years ago, I was driving on the highway. I recall being tired, and at one point, I veered into the lane beside me, cutting off another car. I regained control and brought the car back to my path. I looked over to see the driver of the other car yelling at me while displaying both his middle fingers. As I've done before, I apologized because it was my fault. He couldn't hear me, but I mouthed the words, so it was apparent I was sorry. I took responsibility for my mistake. That is enough for most people.

But not this time. He drove behind me, holding a very close distance to my bumper so as not to lose me. With the work I do teaching violence prevention, I knew to not engage and provoke him, and I try to follow my advice as best I can. Anyway, he followed me all the way to a store where I felt it was safe to get out of my vehicle since there were lots of people to witness what may or may not happen. I got out and stood on my side of the car in a nonthreatening manner. He jumped out of his vehicle, began approaching me aggressively and began yelling so everyone could hear, "You cut me off, asshole! What the fuck?" Without hesitation, I said, "Asshole? That's the third time today someone's called me that, including my wife!" He stopped in his tracks, and his demeanor changed right there and then. He even began laughing. We exchanged a smile, and I again apologized.

Now, a few points here. I used humor to de-escalate. Humor can be a valuable tool in verbal de-escalation, but one that needs to be strategic. Humor, such as making fun of yourself, can work, but not like the humor we use with our best friends in our day-to-day conversations. I was careful not to challenge or threaten him, but instead, supported what he was thinking. But the caveat is to never assume that since it worked for me that time, I would always use that same strategy.

Every scenario involving confrontation has different people, specific surroundings, distinct variables. A tactic that might work one time might be the worst approach to use tomorrow in the same scenario with someone different. Humor, as all these strategies in the book, is a tool, not a definite solution. You learn where and when to implement one or more. And, if humor is not something that comes naturally to you, don't force it, as it can backfire.

In this case, after I made my joke, he could have said something like, "Yeah, you are an asshole, and I am going ram my fist down your throat!" In that case, I would not have continued to force the use of humor, as I would have recognized it wasn't working. Then I would have jumped to one of the alternative concepts I cover in this book.

ROAD RAGE VIDEOS[9]

I want to reference a blog post I wrote on road rage.

Road rage is a phenomenon most have experienced, whether on the receiving or the delivering end of it. Some people are not even conscious of their road rage. If I asked you how many people have experienced road rage, what would your percentage guess be? 50 percent, 60 percent?

Well, according to Credit Donkey, 80 percent of drivers admit to experiencing road rage over any given year. And to make it even more interesting, the article says that millions express extreme road rage.

Why does road rage draw out such fury, combativeness, and violence from even the most gentle, unassuming people regardless of age, gender, or size? People will turn from their meek, patient, peaceful demeanor to someone Satan would envy.

What is road rage? Road rage is violent anger caused by the stress and frustration involved in driving a motor vehicle in difficult conditions. These behaviors include crude and offensive gestures, verbal taunts, physical risks, or risky driving methods aimed toward another driver.

---

9   https://www.youtube.com/watch?v=KBaqPEAjsGY

Road rage can take many forms, including someone giving you an angry look or gesture, to blocking lane changes or cutting someone off to violence with a weapon. And that weapon might be the car, guns, knives, or anything in their vehicle.

So why is road rage more unique than other scenarios we encounter every day? There are several factors:

- It isolates us in a possession that may have cost us a good deal of money. And to have some stranger cost us money is stressful.
- Many feel protected in their vehicles, which can bring out their bold potential attitude to others, never ever expecting how far someone else might take the scenario.
- For some, it extends their already combative personality.
- And others might just be experiencing a stressful day and are at the mercy of their stress in a 4000-pound weapon.

Think about it. On any average day, you are within feet of thousands of vehicles all travelling at varying speeds, assuming they will all be alert and observing the rules of the road 24/7. But how many times have you come close to experiencing an accident?

Perhaps you were distracted, not feeling well, or there was poor weather? I know just over a week ago, I was on a major highway at 5:30 a.m. and did not see a patch of black ice, which took me spinning across lanes into the center median ditch. It was early in the morning, and it involved no other traffic; otherwise, I could have been injured or harmed others. See when it's our own fault, and no one else is involved, we rarely get violent or yell at ourselves. (Or maybe some of you do!)

Next, you have the aggressive driver on the highway putting many people at risk, so how might you deal with that? Take, for example, this video.[10]

Now it may be clear that the male in the truck is out of control and hazardous to other traffic. The people in the car call 911, which I have no issue with. But many people, when they video an incident like this, make sure the road rager sees the camera, assuming they will stop their dangerous behavior. Usually, it has the opposite result, though. The rager now feels challenged and threatened, becoming even more of a threat to others on the road. Then the male in the car yells that they have a baby on board, thinking the guy will stop driving like a maniac and go, "Wow, you have a baby on board? My apologies sir. I will stop now!" You're asking someone in a very heightened stage of anger, aggression, and a violent mindset to reason. They may also be on drugs, taking away any rational thinking. I have no statistic of proof, but 99 percent of the time, we are nuts to think using reason will work in a scenario like this.

As the video fades out, you hear the driver of the car tell his passenger to get him his gun. Now, who knows what could have transpired if the scenario went further. As for these witnesses, they are not in the "wrong" for wanting to help, but I worry that they have put their safety at risk. With the baby in the car, they could have handled it better. It is their safety as well as other innocent people I'm concerned about. The guy in the truck deserves to be arrested and put in jail. Calling 911 was an excellent idea. Just remember to maintain a safe distance behind

---

10 https://www.youtube.com/watch?time_continue=1&v=etMrmvgi2ds&feature=emb_logo

and be sure he does not see you making the call. Once you have made the call, find an exit you can safely take that will remove you from the risk. Once you've made the call, you've done your job. Let the police handle it from there.

Often people will ask what to do if they're confronted. Should they get out of their car or remain in it if someone aggressively gets out and approaches? As always, I say, "Maybe or maybe not." That answer is not a cop-out. It rests on all the variables of the situation. What might be wise to do one day in a road rage scenario might be foolish to do in another. There are a few variables to consider.

- Are you by yourself, or do you have others in the car with you?
- Where are you? Are you isolated or in a traffic jam and can't exit?
- How many people are in or getting out of the other vehicle?
- Do they have weapons? (You don't know.)
- Who are they? Do they have a violent past? (You don't know.)

Countless variables can influence what your best decision might be. And that it might all take effect so quickly can have a radical effect on your decision-making.

Watch this crazy video:[11]

See in the first video, it turns out staying in the car was the safest decision. But if the window was broken, is he a sitting duck? Or maybe the driver has a gun. There are so many

---

11   https://www.youtube.com/watch?v=QB0AlomPlAY#action=share

variables to consider. What scares me most is when we have our loved ones in the car with us and we base our decisions on ego, aggressiveness, anger, or the "I'll teach him a lesson" attitude.

It is essential to recognize that road rage is one of the more stress filled, serious conflicts one can face. People are in a magnified state of stress that can turn to rage in a split second. Many of the poor decisions made are made during road rage.

CHAPTER 9

WORST-CASE SCENARIO

"Always plan for the fact that no plan ever
goes according to plan."
—Simon Sinek

S o, you entered a conflict that appeared to be circumstantial. Your body language was passive, you were nice and friendly; you were asking probing questions to resolve the alleged issue at hand, you listened, you gave options, *but* they are still in your face.

All precontact cues, indications, words, and tone they use indicate they will harm you. I told you this book is not about training the physical side of violence prevention. My later book will address that, but what I will offer you here are the strategies to best set yourself up for a physical response after you have run out of other options. You are now in a position where you believe you can legally, morally, and ethically defend yourself. We said earlier that conflict only goes one of three ways.

1) You part ways with a solution.
2) They will strike you first.
3) You will hit them first.

Number one is not an option at this point. Understand that you can end up attempting verbal de-escalation too long, to where you get struck, slammed to the ground, have a weapon used against you, or are harmed. At some point, you need to make that decision of striking first or hope they do not attack you. If you wait, their attack might be just one strike, and it could be over. It is difficult to make the decision to strike, and if you have zero experience physical violence, you may be in unchartered territory. Once you fight back, remember this.

- You did not want this conflict.
- You have no desire to defend yourself with physical force.
- You attempted every single strategy you could to avoid this.

Now is the time to recall what is important in your life.

The favorable news is that, since you attempted to de-escalate the other person and they have targeted you for violence, your assailant is likely thinking:

- You are weak and vulnerable.
- There is no way to stop them, and
- They can control and dominate you.

How are these an advantage to you? If they consider you weak and vulnerable, excellent. Because when an aggressor uses violence, they target those they feel superior to. What that means is they conclude there is nothing you can do to stop them so they don't prepare to fight you the way they might for, say, a sanctioned sporting event where both have trained, eaten healthy, taken their Flintstone vitamins, then met in the center of the ring. No, they will threaten you in an overconfident nature, never believing you will defend yourself. Your perceived vulnerability offers you an advantage because they will never see your defense coming. They will step in with their hands down, arrogant with their face displayed and provide you with several vulnerable targets on their body.

See, it is never 100 percent guaranteed, but most people will never pick a "fight" with someone whom they think can beat them. And because you did not attempt to take some badass martial arts stance or tell them to "back off" or else, there is no reason for them to get braced for your defense. In an MMA fight or boxing match, there are rules, and while there are still nerves and fear, they are in an agreed-upon event. In targeted violence, there is a considerably different mindset. They may target you to satisfy their desire to harm you. Therefore, you use all the previous strategies. In a worst-case scenario, you want all the odds in your favor to get home:

- Your passive stance does not reveal any fighting ability.
- Your movement and holding a safe distance will provide you with the opportunity to intercept any attack they might launch. Again, if you know what to look for.
- Your body language is not challenging, and if there are witnesses in the distance or close by who do not hear the words being said, they may see from your body language how you did not want to fight. In targeted violence, the other person's body language would tell any witnesses they are the aggressor. Again, your body

language can work for you or against you in the case that whatever happens ends up in front of a judge with you needing to explain your actions.

If all else has failed, before preparing to defend yourself, if the option to run like hell presents itself, take it! Even with stacking the odds in your favor, there are no guarantees for you or the other person. So, if you can run to a safe location, that is optimal. All this depends on the multitude of variables. Things that can affect your options are:

- You have your child or kids with you, so you can't run and leave them there.
- You may have someone with you who cannot run, like a grandparent for example.
- You have an injury, hindering you from escaping.
- You may have a loved one who is limiting you from leaving because of their becoming aggressive back to the other person, and you don't want to leave them where they may be hurt.

I would love to give you a specific answer to any conflict, but that would be dishonest. Violence is chaos, fear, the unknown. All you can do is your best to avoid, handle, or set yourself up for the strongest chance of survival.

CHAPTER 10

SEXUAL ASSAULT

*Know when to implement sniper mode
in your communication strategies!*

———————————

Sexual assault regarding conflict resolution technically could have fit under the Worst-Case Scenario chapter, but I felt it required its own chapter. This topic is most important to me and the one I have focused on for the past twenty-five years. Having worked with over 250,000 women, the strategies in this book are monumental in helping people avoid sexual assault.

Sexual assault fits under targeted conflict. Not impossible, but rarely will you be able to talk a rapist out of sexually assaulting you. The verbal strategies in this book are one's best chance of setting up your survival if avoidance is impossible. Much of what I will point out goes against conventional instruction but will add to your options in handling targeted rape.

Factors that put one at a disadvantage include:

- You may have been the focus of the rapist for a long time, so they are familiar with your daily routines, where you work, or where you like to hang out.

- Domestic violence is prevalent, so the abuser also knows the person, how they behave, their psychology, their weaknesses, etc.

This book is not an in-depth look at the psychology, behavioral, or emotional aspects of sexual assault and rape, but with training beyond what you read here, the strategies I will inform you about offer a higher chance of success.

I must point out the strategies here are not necessarily easy for anyone but may be particularly challenging for someone who has been in an abusive relationship for years. It is too simplistic to tell someone to implement them if they have not sought the proper professional help with their history of abuse and assault.

But one step in healing from the trauma is education, and I hope this advice might help with that. Someone who has not faced a history of abuse may also face challenges in implementing these strategies.

To recap a few points: Recall that someone who targets you believes you're weak and vulnerable, so your perceived vulnerability is your greatest asset and one that fits with the verbal strategies offered. This is where the strategy is often taught of yelling, "back off!" immediately can fail. In that moment of fear, you're trying to convince someone who deems you as weak that you're strong. And it is *not* strategic to foretell someone that you will or might attempt to fight back. That only increases their awareness of your intentions. Telling them through your body language and words that you will fight back may quicken and escalate their level of attack to either shut you up or to meet your threats and commands. Yelling can work in a public place or in a lower level threat where someone is merely rude, obnoxious, or looking for a physical encounter. But where do most sexual assaults take place? In isolated locations where no one may hear you.

Sexual assaults take place in very close quarters. The person needs to gain the closest proximity to make avoidance impossible. If a physical response is your only option, lure them in as close as possible. To attempt a strike with them a few feet from you is very risky. Not impossible, but difficult. It might sound counterproductive to want them in close, but this is where you have the best chance of survival. Unless you're running away, distance is not your friend once you make the decision to fight back.

The strategies we've explored of being nice, kind, and helpful offer an attacker no reason to heighten their guard to your intentions. Now, there are countless ways this all may transpire.

If one is attacked with no dialogue or warning, the reaction *must* be physical, so it does not fit into conflict resolution with dialogue first.

You may not know at first if you've been targeted. The person may be interested in a consensual relationship. So, if it is becoming physical beyond what is acceptable to you, you can still be nice in saying you're not interested. You're communicating you're not comfortable. They should respect that and stop. As Gavin DeBecker, the author of the amazing book, *The Gift of*

Fear, says, "The word no is a complete sentence."[12] But, if you've been targeted, it won't matter what you say.

To yell and scream may trigger that person into an immediate attack. As we've noted repeatedly, any strategy can work sometimes, but you never really know. So, having options is preferable. If you've established that the situation has gone beyond what's acceptable to you and you have told them you're not interested, but they continue, you need to use your body language, words, and tone to mask your intentions to fight back. They may be direct and disgusting with their language, leaving little wonder to their intentions. Recall what we said about words earlier? They are just words. They only have power over you if you let them.

The goal, once you know there is no chance of de-escalating, is to use their strategy against them. If they're preparing for a physical fight, don't give them the body language, words, and tone they would expect to see. Be nice, make it about them. If you say things like, "Please don't hurt me!" or "I have a family. Please don't do this!" it will not gain any empathy from them if they're a sociopath or psychopath, which is highly likely in this type of scenario.

Instead, say things that will appeal to their ego without raising their guard to your intention to fight back. Use your body language, words, and tone to indicate you're a willing participant. Many will make the point that you have consented if you show you're willing. Again, this is a strategy you implement only after your confident, but polite rebukes have not been accepted or

---

12   Gavin De Becker, *The Gift of Fear: Survival Signals That Protect Us from Violence* (London: Bloomsbury, 2010), 197

heard with empathy, once it is apparent that they will assault or rape you, you are not consenting; you are *appearing* to consent to survive. You can offer the appearance of consent in many ways if it appears real to them.

I understand this sounds opposite to what you really want, but you need to understand that just telling them what you don't want has no effect on them. Just telling a rapist to back off is one very limited strategy. They're a rapist and intend to take whatever they want. You need to make them believe they'll get what they want, and when the moment presents itself, you react with the ferocity and will to survive that they never saw or heard in your communication. This all ties back to the reasons mentioned over and over about getting home.

THE CONFLICT IS OVER...
OR APPEARS TO BE

"It's never over 'till it's over!"
—Winston Churchill

Imagine you have cleared up the conflict at hand. Either you came to an understanding that resulted in both parties appearing content with the outcome, or you resolved it with a civil agreement to disagree.

Whatever the end, it looks like both people can step away without violence. One serious mistake some people make is letting their guard down too soon. They relax, turn their back to walk away, and then get struck from behind, never seeing it coming.

This happens more than you might think. Just minutes before, you may have both been yelling at each other. Exit with caution and your eyes on what was a threat moments before.

Please keep your eyes on that person until you're at a safe distance or have come to a safer location.

Their acquiescence may have been a setup to drop your guard. I hate to say it, but some are skilled at appearing to have cooled down, and you might even swear they had by their body language, words, and tone—but you never know.

Another caution is to avoid shaking the other person's hand at the end of any confrontation. It may seem polite, but you can be polite without having to touch them or get within proximity. If they attempt to shake your hand, I might suggest you say you have a cold flu or even that you're a germaphobe.

With the slightest physical contact, you're providing them with an opportunity to grab you, pull you in, and strike you. If they're adamant about shaking your hand as the last step, that is ultimately up to you but understand the potential consequences and prepare yourself if they attempt physical harm.

CONCLUSION

Conflict resolution has many layers, but you now have the strategies to Disarm Daily Conflict.

The critical message is understanding the costs to not only you, but to those you love, and even the one you conflict with. The first step is to do some honest inner reflection on how you dealt with conflict in the past. Analyze where you handled it well, and where you can improve.

The biggest challenge is not the person you conflict with but managing yourself. If you can't manage your own emotions, how can you expect to de-escalate someone else.

I encourage you to read the book more than once or refer to chapters of interest. Please reach out to us with your questions, or to share your personal story.

Keep SAFE!
Chris Roberts

APPENDIX A:
SAFE 101 VERBAL
DE-ESCALATION CHECKLIST

1) Avoid confrontation and conflict. If you aren't there, it can't take place.

2) If you are face to face with someone in any dispute, death hovers. It may arise by accident, circumstance, or variable error.

3) Remember: you do not know the individual in front of you, their psychological state of mind, or what they may be capable of.

4) Conflict only goes one of three ways. You part ways, they strike you first, or you hit them first.

5) Conflict is circumstantial or targeted. It may start off as circumstantial and change to targeted based on the body language, words, and tone used.

6) Remember the costs to you, your family, and the other person before reacting.

7) Always be nice, do not challenge, do not threaten, do not command, do not tell them they are wrong, make it about them.

8) Understand the power of saying, "I am Sorry!" Say you are sorry when you've made a mistake.

9) Listen with empathy to understand before speaking.

10) "How can I help you?" is an excellent opening question to determine the issue.

11) Words are just words with only the meaning you attach to them.

12) Exit keeping awareness heightened until you get home.

ACKNOWLEDGEMENTS

There are a few individuals I would like to acknowledge for their support, help, and contributions to this book and my work with SAFE International. Foremost is my closest friend, Richard Dimitri, who has been my biggest influence in how to look at violence prevention from more than a self-defense perspective. More than that, his knowledge, teachings, and continual support have influenced this book and saved and changed countless lives around the world. He has been my voice more times than I can count, and my travel companion more than he has wanted. I will always treasure the friendship.

I would also like to thank Jim Armstrong, my Australian friend, who is one of the most amazing, caring, empathetic human beings I have ever met and a world-class instructor who can be seen in this book. Few people can make me laugh so hard, so, thanks for that.

Thanks to my editor – Beacon Point LLC.

Special thanks to Audra Kay for her contributions to the book and her husband, Marc Joseph. Both are dear friends who have always supported my efforts in teaching violence prevention.

Also, thanks to some of my SAFE friends and partners through this journey whom I consider dear friends: Jeff Phillips, Steven O'Connor, and Julian McQuade in Australia; Thorsten Bruchhauser in Germany; and my dear friend Bill Stedman.

Thanks to Pamela Armitage for bringing a new, often neglected level of education on Trauma into our teachings. In addition, all the instructors who represent SAFE International making the world a little safer. While there are far too many to mention and I fear I might miss out on a few, you know who you are.

And thanks to Darren Norton and Russell Jarmesty for sharing their thoughts on conflict resolution.

CHRIS ROBERTS BIO

In an effort to provide people with the tools to disarm any conflict one may face in their daily lives, Chris Roberts started SAFE International™, providing self-defense and violence prevention education in Canada then expanded to several countries around the world. Since its start in 1994, his organization has taught more than 250,000 people in schools, corporations, families, martial arts clubs, and women's groups. Their self-defense parties have been featured on Global TV in Canada.

Chris knows that a moment of conflict can destroy lives, and the most challenging part for people is to use simple, but effective communication during a conflict to de-escalate the situation. So, he wrote this book to extend the reach of his important message. His expertise and trainings not only teach others how to avoid violence, but he also focuses on the psychological, behavioral, and emotional aspects.

When he isn't working on his business, he enjoys being a coffee snob and "Grampy" to his two granddaughters.

He hopes everyone learns what to do in a conflict so they can get home to what matters most: their family.

WE WOULD LOVE YOUR OPINION

Thank You for Reading My Book!

I appreciate the valuable time you took to read it. I would love your feedback and hearing what you have to say.

I need your input to make the next version of this book and my future books better.

Please leave me a helpful review on Amazon, letting me know what you thought of the book.

Thanks so much and Keep SAFE!!
- Chris Roberts -

NEXT STEPS

In case you want a more in-depth, step-by-step look at violence prevention, self-defense, or certification please visit www.safe101.education and www.safeinternational.biz

If you are interested in bringing our world-class education to individuals, schools, corporations, families, seniors, or anyone deemed vulnerable please visit http://safe101.education/courses/

Or perhaps you want to be certified to bring this lifesaving education to those you need it most, please visit http://safe101.education/courses/safecertification/

WANT SOME FREE STUFF?
We would love to send you lots of free tips, videos, and other valuable life-saving resources.
All you have to do is subscribe to our email list at www.safe101.education

Printed in Great Britain
by Amazon

38809836R00078